P9-DWR-523
KODOCHA
SANA'S STAGE

Vol. 6

Written and Illustrated by Miho Obana
English Adaptation by Sarah Dyer

Story and Art - Miho Obana
Translator - Amy Forsyth
English Adaption - Sarah Dyer
Editor - Amy C. Kaemon
Retouch and Lettering - Marnie Echols
Cover Layout - Anna Kernbaum

Senior Editor - Julie Taylor
Managing Editor - Jill Freshney
Production Manager - Jennifer Miller
Art Director - Matthew Alford
Director of Editorial - Jeremy Ross
VP of Production & Manufacturing - Ron Klamert
President & C.O.O. - John Parker
Publisher - Stuart Levy

Email: editor@TOKYOPOP.com
Come visit us online at www.TOKYOPOP.com

A TOKYOPOP® Manga
TOKYOPOP® is an imprint of Mixx Entertainment Inc.
5900 Wilshire Blvd. Suite 2000, Los Angeles, CA 90036

"KODOMO NO OMOCHA"

ISBN: 1-59182-182-7

First TOKYOPOP® printing: April 2003

10 9 8 7 6 5 4 3 2

Printed in the USA

Vol. 6

CONTENTS

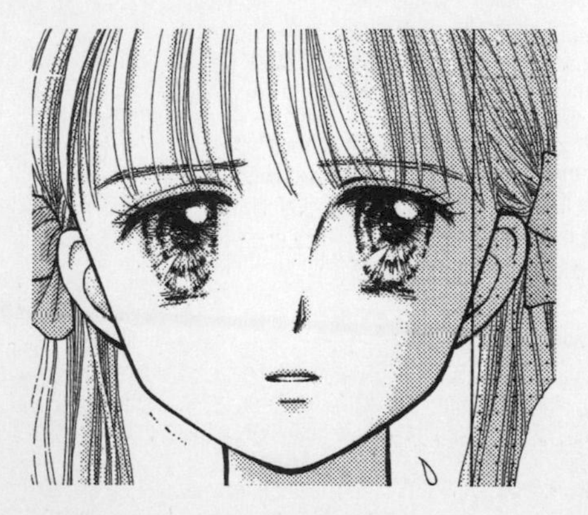

UR CHARACTERS
SANA KURATA
A POPULAR CHILD STAR WHO'S TRYING TO JUST BE A REGULAR 7TH GRADE GIRL.
REI SAGAMI
SANA'S MANAGER.
AKITO HAYAMA
SANA'S CLASSMATE AND CLOSE FRIEND. REALLY INTO KARATE.
NAOZUMI KAMURA
A VERY POPULAR CHILD STAR. HAS A THING FOR SANA.
FUKA MATSUI
GREW UP IN OSAKA, BUT MOVED BACK THIS YEAR. SHE AND SANA ARE GOOD FRIENDS.
TSUYOSHI SASAKI
ANOTHER CLASSMATE AND FRIEND. NICE GUY, BUT WHAT A TEMPER!
MARIKO KURATA
SANA'S MOM, A FAMOUS WRITER.

WHAT'S HAPPENED SO FAR:

SANA IS A POPULAR CHILD STAR WHO APPEARS ON TV — IN SHOWS, MOVIES AND ADS. LAST YEAR HER MOTHER WROTE A BOOK REVEALING THAT SHE'D FOUND SANA ABANDONED ON A PARK BENCH AND ADOPTED HER. SANA PANICKED — SHE WAS AFRAID SHE'D HAVE TO LEAVE MARIKO. BUT WHEN SHE FINALLY MET HER BIRTH MOTHER, SHE TOLD HER <AND MARIKO> THAT MARIKO IS HER "REAL" MOTHER, AND EVERYTHING SETTLED DOWN. BUT THINGS CAN NEVER GO SMOOTHLY IN SANA'S LIFE — SHE STARTED JUNIOR HIGH AND BECAME GOOD FRIENDS WITH A NEW GIRL, FUKA — ONLY TO FIND OUT THAT AKITO WAS FUKA'S FIRST KISS, TOO! IT TURNED OUT TO BE NOTHING, BUT THINGS STILL WEREN'T SETTLED BETWEEN SANA AND AKITO. WHEN SANA AGREED TO STAR IN A BIG MOVIE, SHE HAD TO LEAVE FOR THREE MONTHS OF LOCATION SHOOTING. AKITO CAME TO SEE HER OFF, AND SAID HE HAD SOMETHING TO TELL HER...BUT ONCE AGAIN, HE COULDN'T SAY ANYTHING.

ON LOCATION, SANA FINDS HERSELF THINKING ABOUT AKITO CONSTANTLY — ALTHOUGH SHE ISN'T SURE WHY. SHE'S LOOKING FORWARD TO WRAPPING UP AND GETTING BACK HOME, WHEN A TABLOID PRINTS A MADE-UP STORY CLAIMING THAT SANA AND HER CO-STAR, NAOZUMI, ARE ROMANTICALLY INVOLVED! SANA IS ANNOYED, BUT THAT'S NOTHING COMPARED TO NAOZUMI'S CRAZY FANS, WHO ARE FURIOUS AND ATTACK SANA...

キャアアアア
NAOZUMI KAMURA:
HAS HE GONE MAD?!
NAOZUMI ATTACKS FANS
!!
ka-pow!!
あああ
OH, NO !!
NAOZUMI!! NOOOOO!!
DON'T GO MAD!
NO
NO
たっくる

NAOZUMI, GET A GRIP!!
CALM DOWN!
ひょい
どさーっ
わあああっ
NAOZUMI'S SCARY!
NAOZUMI... DON'T BE SO ANGRY!
WE'RE SORR-
SORRY? YOU THINK YOU CAN JUST SAY, "SORRY"?
WHAT THE HELL WERE YOU THINKING?!
HUH ?!
TELL ME!!
HE'S USUALLY SO CALM... THIS IS SCARY!!
NAOZUMI!
STOP IT! I'M FINE, OKAY?

NAO-ZUMI'S SO MEAN!
DIDN'T I SAY THIS WAS A BAD IDEA?
UH, NO...
GET BACK HERE!
NAOZUMI!
SANA?!
WHAT'S GOING ON?
OH! MR. MAEDA! NAOZUMI'S JUST A LITTLE EXCITED, THAT'S ALL...
I'LL GET YOU !!
I'LL RIP YOU INTO PIECES!
NAO! YOU NEED TO CALM DOWN.
SANA! SANA, ARE YOU ALL RIGHT?
UM... YEAH...
ANGRY BLUES
HE'S FINE ...
SANA, WHAT HAP-PENED ?!

SOME OF MY FANS ...
...THEY AMBUSHED ME.
WHAT ?!
DON'T ACT CASUAL.
BUT SERIOUSLY, I'M FINE.
!!
WHA?!
AH-
AAAAAAAAH!!!
OWWWW!!
MY LEG! AAAHHH ...
SANA!
LET'S TAKE HER BACK!
OW...
SHE'S PRETTY BADLY BANGED UP...
HER LEG MIGHT EVEN BE BROKEN.
YOU SHOULD TAKE HER TO SEE A DOCTOR.

SANA, I'M SO SORRY. I SHOULD BE WATCHING OVER YOU...
I WAS ENJOYING A HOT BATH WITH THE MONKEYS ...
OH!
I'M FINE.
NOTHING CAN HURT ME!
WE'RE OFF TO THE DOCTOR'S. LATER!
IS THERE A DOCTOR NEARBY...?
MR. SAGAMI, TAKE THIS MAP.
SANA'S REALLY HURT.
WHAT ABOUT THE MOVIE?
WE MIGHT HAVE TO REPLACE HER.

CLINIC
WELL, SHE'S GOT A LOT OF DEEP BRUISES...
...AND A HAIRLINE FRACTURE IN HER LEFT LEG.
DRAGGED OUT OF BED
HER LEG IS BROKEN?
WELL, NOT EXACTLY... IT'S CRACKED.
SHE'S GOT A COUPLE OF TINY CRACKS ON HER SHINBONE ...
FRACTURE MEANS "BREAK" OR "CRACK." DIDN'T YOU KNOW THAT?
CRACKS, HUH?
THIS SUCKS...
ズキ ズキ

①
Obana's Incoherent Babbling
Hello! It's me, Miho Obana. Thank you for sticking with us this far!
Speaking of far, can you believe this is book 6? Half the time, I think "Woo-hoo! I'm past the halfway mark!" and the other half, I think, "I'm already halfway done?"
From this book on, the tone of Kodocha changes quite a bit. I was pretty nervous writing it! But all things change in real life, so I couldn't just keep on writing the same old thing. Thinking about how much people grow and change, it's happy/sad, fun/heartbreaking, and exciting/depressing all at once!
This is "Obana-ese," and it doesn't really mean anything, so don't worry if you can't understand it.
And by the way, my cat is growing up, too.
PLEASE READ "THE ISLAND OF CATS." *
She's getting to be as big as a dog!
*EDITOR'S NOTE: ANOTHER MIHO OBANA COMIC BOOK.

THE CLINIC, THAT NIGHT
SANA, I THINK YOU'RE GOING TO HAVE TO QUIT THE FILM.
WHAT A SHAME!
HUH?
WHAT'RE YOU BABBLING ABOUT?
I CAN STILL DO IT!
IT'S NOT LIKE MAKO RUNS AROUND, OR JUMPS... SHE JUST WALKS AROUND VERY SLOWLY.
THAT'S NO PROBLEM! SO I CAN STILL DO IT...
PLUS, I SAVED MY FACE!
WE CAN COVER BRUISES WITH MAKEUP!
NO WAY!
WHAT IF YOU GET HURT? I CAN'T LET YOU...
REI! I'M GOING TO DO IT!
ONCE I'VE MADE UP MY MIND TO DO SOMETHING, I NEVER QUIT!
I'M STUBBORN LIKE A SNAKE!
SANA!

SANA! I WANTED YOU TO BE IN THIS MOVIE MORE THAN ANYTHING...
...BUT YOU CANNOT KEEP WORKING WITH CRACKS IN YOUR LEG!
CRACKS, SCHMACKS! I'M FINE! EVEN WHEN MY FACE DRIES UP AND CRACKS, I WON'T CARE!
OH, DEAR!
MY HANDS ARE ALL CRACKED!
LOOK AT MRS. SHIMURA—SHE'S ALL CRACKED AND WRINKLY, BUT SHE SEEMS PRETTY LIVELY.
SANA, WRINKLES ARE NOTHING LIKE A CRACKED BONE!
REI, SERIOUSLY—I REALLY WANT TO DO THIS MOVIE. IT'S IMPORTANT TO ME, TOO.
PLEASE? I PROMISE NOT TO OVERDO IT.
AND I'LL TELL YOU IF I START TO FEEL BAD...
OKAY?
PROMISE!
......
ピチチチ…

②

The Allure of the Beauty Salon

I've started getting these strange phone calls inviting me to come and try out a beauty salon. What's this all about? I don't even know these ladies who are suddenly calling me! So I just hang up.

They're always telling me about their different treatments - waxes, facials, weight loss counseling. Maybe I'd care if I wanted to just be beautiful! (Hee hee!)

The funny thing is, they're so belligerent about it...

DON'T KNOW HER
YOU'RE FILTHY!
YOU LOOK UGLY!
BWAHAHA!

YOU'RE ALL HAIRY!
COME IN NOW!

...At least, that's what I feel like they're saying.

NO, THANK YOU...
I'M MUCH TOO BUSY.

So I just hang up on them!

③ to be continued...

HI, EVERYONE! I'M FINE! IT'S JUST A BAD BRUISE!
I CAN WORK, NO PROBLEM! I'LL DO MY BEST.
REALLY? THAT'S A RELIEF...
NO, IT ISN'T! SANA, DOESN'T IT HURT?
DON'T WORRY, ASAKO. I'LL BE CAREFUL.
I'M SORRY I MADE YOU ALL WORRY!
SANA, NAOZUMI'S BEEN WORRIED, TOO.
HE'S BEEN ACTING REALLY DOWN.
COME ON, NAO... STOP BEING SO GLOOMY!
......
I ...I'VE HAD... ENOUGH OF THIS...
I... I QUIT...
WHAT? WHAT'RE YOU SAYING?

YOU HAVE SO MANY GREAT FANS OUT THERE. DON'T LET A FEW CRAZY ONES RUIN THINGS FOR YOU.
I SAID, ENOUGH!
I QUIT!
NAOZUMI...
SANA... SHE'S THE REASON...
CLAP YOUR HANDS! CLAP! CLAP!
...I WANTED TO BE IN SHOW BUSINESS...
I CAN'T STAND IT.
I QUIT.
ギィー
DID YOU SAY QUIT?
I WON'T LET YOU DO THAT, NAOZUMI.
SANA!

MR. MAEDA, COULD I TALK TO NAOZUMI ALONE?
SURE ...
I'M GOING TO KEEP WORKING EVEN HARDER...
...AND SO SHOULD YOU!
DON'T YOU DARE QUIT ON MY ACCOUNT!
YEAH, I'VE GOT SOME BRUISES... SO WHAT? I'M FINE!
YOU CAN'T JUST SAY I'M FINE AND FORGET ABOUT IT!
I HATE THEM ALL!
THOSE GIRLS...AND THOSE REPORTERS!
WELL, THAT'S JUST THE WAY REPORTERS AND MAGAZINES ARE. YOU CAN'T DO ANYTHING ABOUT IT.
ALL THEY CARE ABOUT IS SALES.
SANA'S OLD LADY HAIRSTYLE FROM VOLUME FIVE
AND THOSE GIRLS ONLY ACTED THAT WAY BECAUSE THEY LIKED YOU TOO MUCH.
YOU BEING SO ANGRY AT THEM FOR IT IS KIND OF SAD.
茶

THEY DID THIS TO ME BECAUSE THEY WANTED ME TO QUIT WORKING WITH YOU.
THE BEST REVENGE I CAN HAVE ON THEM IS TO KEEP GOING...
...DO MY BEST, AND APPEAR IN THE MOVIE BY YOUR SIDE.
HOW CAN YOU BE SO CALM?! WHY AREN'T YOU ANGRY AT THEM, TOO?!
ARE YOU NUTS? OF COURSE I'M ANGRY AT THEM!
THOSE LITTLE BRATS! I'D LIKE TO CRACK EVERY BONE IN THEIR BODIES!
BUT I CAN'T. SO I'LL HAVE TO THINK OF SOMETHING EVEN BETTER...
BETTER...?
SO THAT'S MY PLAN! AND NOW THAT I HAVE EVEN MORE REASON TO WORK HARD, THE MOVIE WILL BE BETTER! I CAN KILL TWO BIRDS WITH ONE STONE!
THEY'LL GET THEIRS...
......
SANA...SHE'S INCREDIBLE.
NO MATTER WHAT HAPPENS, SHE FINDS A POSITIVE SIDE TO IT.
IT'S AMAZING...
SANA... I CAN'T BE LIKE YOU...

MY MOM ONCE TOLD ME, "WHEN YOU FEEL LIKE THINGS ARE AT THEIR WORST, TRY TO ENJOY YOURSELF THE MOST."
I DIDN'T UNDERSTAND HER BACK THEN, BUT I THINK SHE WAS TALKING ABOUT A TIME LIKE THIS.
I CAN'T CHANGE WHAT HAPPENED,
SO I'LL JUST MAKE THE BEST OF IT!
ぱーっ
YOU TOO, NAOZUMI!
C'MON! BE HAPPY!
I SEE YOUR POINT, SANA...
...BUT IT'S JUST NOT THAT EASY.
ぶつぶつ
COME ON!!
ガタッ
BESIDES, WHO WANTED ME TO TAKE THIS JOB IN THE FIRST PLACE?
YOU! SO IF I'M GONNA DO MY BEST AND KEEP WORKING EVEN THOUGH I'M HURTING, THERE'S NO WAY I'M GONNA LET YOU OFF THE HOOK...
ズキッ
AHH!
SANA!

ARE YOU OKAY?
SANA, IS YOUR LEG REALLY JUST BRUISED?
オロ
オロ
WHAT? OF COURSE IT IS!
STOP WORRYING.
フフフ…
THIS IS NOTHING!
COMPARED TO THE PAIN OF GIVING BIRTH, IT'S JUST A SCRATCH.
ゼー
ズキズキ
HOW WOULD SHE KNOW ...?
NAOZUMI.
...
WE'VE COME THIS FAR.
LET'S GET THE JOB DONE!
......
NOD

SANA...
MAKE SURE YOU KEEP SANA'S BANDAGE OUT OF THE SHOT.
RIGHT!
YEAH, DUH...
HOW'S THE LIGHT-ING?
READY.
SCENE 61...TEST SHOT.
LET'S GO, EVERY-BODY!
WHAT DO YOU MEAN? YOUR BROTHER...
HE-
E
E
YOWCH!!

WHA-?
SANA, ARE YOU ALL-RIGHT?
SORRY!
LET'S TRY AGAIN, OKAY?
...SANA...
SCENE 63.
ACTION!
SHE'S ...
...SO STRONG.

SANA, ARE YOU SURE YOU'RE OKAY? DO YOU NEED TO STOP FOR THE DAY?
NO, I'M FINE.
HERE, HAVE SOME TEA AND REST FOR A MINUTE.
OKAY, THANKS.
ズキ
ズキ
I FEEL BETTER ALREADY
IT HURTS, BUT I CAN HANDLE IT.
ズキン
I CAN DO IT.
ズキン
MY HEART IS STILL FULL OF STRENGTH!
ズキン
YOU DO YOUR BEST, TOO.
HYA!
AKITO...
...I'M GIVING IT MY ALL...
ズキン
ズキン
フウ...
I COULDN'T DEFEND MYSELF!
MAYBE I SHOULD TAKE KARATE, TOO.
THOSE GIRLS ARE HERE TO APOLOGIZE.
NAOZUMI?
HUH?
THEY SEEM TO FEEL REALLY BAD ABOUT WHAT THEY DID.
I GUESS THEY REALIZED WHAT HAPPENED.
I'M NOT THE ONE THEY NEED TO APOLOGIZE TO.
TELL THEM TO GO TELL SANA THEY'RE SORRY.

YOU WANT TO APOLOGIZE TO ME?
DON'T BOTHER.
IT'S NOT GOING TO CHANGE THE FACT THAT YOU HATE ME.
WELL, GUESS WHAT? I HATE YOU, TOO!
SANA, DON'T PROVOKE THEM.
へろ〜〜ん
FORGET SAYING YOU'RE SORRY. JUST WATCH ME IN THE FILM!
I WANT YOU TO SEE HOW HARD I WORK ...
...AND HOW SERIOUS I AM ABOUT WHAT I DO.
MR. SAGAMI,
I HEARD THAT SANA WASN'T FEELING WELL.
WELL... SHE'S RUNNING A FEVER.
I THINK IT'S BECAUSE OF HER LEG.

ハァ
ハァ
GET WELL. GET WELL.
GET WELL.
GET WELL.
うう～ん…
PRAYING
きゅ
A... AKITO... YOU... ...JERK...
ムニャ…
すー

AND NOW WE GO TO THE SET OF MIKIO ONO'S NEW FILM,
MANSION OF WATER.
I DON'T GET IT!
MAKE YOUR MOUTH GO "MMM".
LIKE THIS... MMM-MM.
THE YOUNG CO-STARS HAVE GREAT CHEMISTRY. ON AND OFF THE SET, THEY'RE ALWAYS TOGETHER.
24/7!
OH, LIKE NNNNN?
NO, NO - MMMMM.
NNN
NNN
HERE, WATCH ME. MMMM.
I SEE! NNNN?
NO, TRY AGAIN... MMMMM.
I DID IT!
SO IT WAS MMMMM, AFTER ALL.
JUST LIKE I TOLD YOU!
DON'T THEY LOOK GREAT TOGETHER?!
WHAT A CUTE COUPLE!
I ALWAYS THOUGHT SANA GOT ALONG GREAT WITH YOU, BUT SHE SEEMS SO COM-FORTABLE WITH THAT GUY...
HEY, DID YOU READ THIS ARTICLE?
IT LOOKS LIKE THEY REALLY ARE GOING OUT!
F. TeeNS

映画 水の館 撮影快調
倉田紗南
加村直澄
恋人宣言
YOU GUYS! IS THIS FOR REAL?
キーン
コーン
I SAW THE TV REPORT... AND NOW THIS ARTICLE...
SERIOUSLY, IS SANA GOIN' OUT WITH THAT KAMURA GUY?
WELL, SANA HASN'T SAID ANYTHING TO ME ABOUT IT ...
ME NEI-THER.
...BUT THAT ARTICLE SAYS THEY ANNOUNCED IT...
COULD THEY HAVE HOOKED UP WHEN THEY WENT ON LOCATION ?
MAYBE NAOZUMI'S MANAGER WOULDN'T LET THEM ANNOUNCE IT UNTIL NOW...
F.TEENS
THE ARTICLE IS TRUE. SANA IS GOING OUT WITH HIM.
WHAT?!
WHO?
WAIT A MINUTE!
YOU'RE...
ボーーン

MR. BIG EYE-BROWS?
MR. BIG EYE-LASHES...
...MR. BIG OL' BUTT?
IS THAT RIGHT?
I KNOW, YOU'RE MR. EYEBROWS-EYELASHES-BIG-BIG-NOSEBLEEDS! HA HA!!
I'M ISHIDA!!
BEFORE SANA LEFT, I ASKED HER IF SHE'D GO OUT WITH ME.
BUT SHE TOLD ME SHE COULDN'T. SHE SAID SHE WAS ALREADY GOING OUT WITH NAOZUMI.
KEEPS TO HIM-SELF AND HAS NO IDEA WHAT'S BEEN GOING ON
WHAAAT!?
HOLD ON, ARE YOU SERIOUS?
I THINK YOU'RE LYIN'!
I'M TELLING THE TRUTH!
DO THESE LOOK LIKE THE EYES OF SOMEONE WHO'S LYING?
HEY!
STOP LOOKING AT MY EYE-BROWS!
I SAID TO LOOK IN MY EYES!
DAMMIT
DID SANA REALLY TELL YOU THAT? SHE'S GOIN' OUT WITH KAMURA?
I SWEAR!

……
ポイ
I CAN'T FIGURE HER OUT! I THOUGHT SHE WASN'T INTERESTED IN BOYS YET.
I TOLD AKITO I'D HELP HIM GET WITH SANA.
映画
SO MUCH FOR THAT IDEA!
POOR AKITO...
WHAT ARE YOU TALKING ABOUT?
morn— —ing.
ず
ざっ
AKITO, YOU SHOULD SEE...
NO!!
YOU CAN'T LET HIM...
OH, THAT. I SAW IT ALREADY.
MY SISTER READS THAT STUFF.
ずるーっ

BUT, AKITO ...
IT'S FINE... I DON'T CARE WHAT SHE DOES.
HANG ON!
I THOUGHT YOU REALLY CARED ABOUT SANA!
YEAH!
NO...I DON'T.
I DON'T CARE ANYMORE.
TSUYOSHI, I TOLD YOU ONCE THAT SANA JUST TAKES IN ALL THE SAD-LOOKING STRAY ANIMALS SHE FINDS...
SHE TOOK ME IN...AND MAYBE I JUST GOT USED TO HER TAKING CARE OF ME...
BUT NOW THAT SHE'S NOT AROUND...
...I JUST DON'T CARE...

IF SHE WANTS TO GO OUT WITH THAT CREEP NAOZUMI, THAT'S FINE WITH ME.
AKITO... ARE YOU SURE...?
YES.
I'M DONE TALKING ABOUT IT, OKAY?
HEY, AKITO! GOOD MORNING!
BUT... AKITO LOOKS SO LONELY...
SANA, YOU IDIOT...
I GUESS IT'S TRUE... "OUT OF SIGHT, OUT OF MIND."
YEAH...
HE CAN'T EVEN CALL AND TALK TO HER.
IT'S BEEN 2 MONTHS...
I GUESS HE'S GOTTEN USED TO HER NOT BEING AROUND.

HEY, AKI!
WAIT UP!
WHAT'S SHE WANT?
はっ
UH, AKITO...
WHAT NOW?
LET ME GUESS—YOU NEED ME TO PRETEND TO BE YOUR DAD?
DON'T PUSH IT.
NO, DUMMY!
IT'S JUST... I WAS TALKIN' TO ONE OF MY FRIENDS FROM OSAKA.
TAKAISHI AND SHIZU ARE GETTIN' ALONG NOW.
I WAS AFRAID THEY WERE HAVIN' TROUBLE 'CAUSE OF ME, AFTER THAT VISIT...
...SO I WAS HAPPY TO HEAR IT.
ARE YOU SURE YOU WEREN'T UPSET?
NO! I WAS HAPPY!
FOR REAL!

I KNOW I'M NOT SANA...
...BUT, AKI...
I KNOW YOU WERE ONLY PRETENDIN' TO BE MY BOYFRIEND...
AND... I WAS THINKIN' HOW MUCH YOU HELPED ME OUT...
...BUT I THOUGHT YOU WERE REALLY GREAT... AND I WAS WONDERIN'...
...WOULD YOU BE MY BOYFRIEND ... FOR REAL?

TAKE 5!
HERE.
SANA, YOU OKAY?
I'M FINE, I'M FINE.
EVEN WITH THIS HEAT WAVE?
I'M BOILING UP!
SHE'S HURTING...
...HER LEG CAN'T HEAL AS LONG AS SHE KEEPS WALKING ON IT...
HANG IN THERE, SANA... YOU CAN DO IT...
...JUST A LITTLE LONGER...
HEY, SANA!
COME WITH ME.
REI, BRING SANA OVER HERE, OKAY?
WHY?
LOOK! MR. ONO LENT ME HIS CELL PHONE.
A PHONE?
YEAH. DIDN'T YOU HAVE A CALL YOU NEEDED TO MAKE?
DIGITAL

YEAH, BUT... I THOUGHT CELL PHONES DIDN'T WORK UP HERE.
I KNOW, BUT I FINALLY FOUND ONE SPECIAL PLACE WHERE YOU CAN GET A SIGNAL!
COOL, HUH?
SEE?
GO OVER THERE. IT'LL WORK JUST FINE.
REALLY?
YUP!
♪ GO AHEAD!
WOW!
THANKS, ASAKO!
HOW COOL!
HE SHOULD BE HOME TODAY...
ピ
SANA! WHO ARE YOU CALLING FIRST?
PROBABLY HER TEACHER.
COOL!
IT WORKED!
HELLO?
IS THIS THE HAYAMA RESIDENCE?
LONG TIME, NO SEE! IT'S ME, SANA!
SHE'S CALLING AKITO...?
NOT EVEN CLOSE...
...

SANA ...?
YEAH, IT'S REALLY ME! HOW ARE YOU?!
OKAY, I HOPE...
I GOT AHOLD OF A PHONE I COULD USE UP HERE!
SO I WANTED TO CALL YOU AND SAY HI!
YEAH, YEAH...
I'M FINE.
OH, AKITO! WHAT WAS IT THAT YOU WANTED TO TALK TO ME ABOUT?
UH...
IT DOESN'T MATTER...
OH, COME ON, WHAT—
HANG ON, I'VE GOT ANOTHER CALL.
OKAY...
HE'S TAKING SO LONG...
HI!
SO, WHO WAS ON THE OTHER LINE?
TSUYOSHI?
OH, FUKA?!
WHAT'S SHE UP TO?

...
WHAT?
OH...
...REALLY?
Y...YEAH, I'M SURPRISED ...
YEAH...
OH, YOU HAVE TO GO?
I SEE. WELL, THEN...
...TELL EVERYONE I SAID HI, OKAY...? ♬
ピ...
SANA, ARE YOU DONE ALREADY?
......

SANA?!
FUKA AND I...
...WE'RE GOING OUT NOW.
SANA, WHAT'S WRONG?
SANA?

OKAY, LET'S GET STARTED!
COME ON EVERY-ONE!
WOW...
...WHAT'S WITH SANA?
HER FACE LOOKS TOTALLY LIFE-LESS!
SHE LOOKS LIKE A REAL GHOST!
IT'S GOOD TO BE IN CHARACTER, BUT...
VANE

ボエー
......
PSST! SANA...
HUH? IS IT MY LINE?
...IT'S NOT LIKE YOU TO FORGET A LINE...
WHAT HAPPENED?
ALL RIGHT! CUT!
SANA?
I'M SORRY...
GO REST FOR A SEC...
SANA, ARE YOU OKAY?
IT...IT'S NOTHING.
COME ON, SANA... WHAT'S UP?
SANA...
DID AKITO SAY SOMETHING TO UPSET YOU?
REALLY, IT'S NOTHING.
LET'S GET BACK. I'VE RESTED ENOUGH.
...DAMMIT, AKITO...
WHAT DID YOU SAY TO HER?

SIX YEARS AGO, AT THE EDGE OF THAT LAKE...
THAT'S WHERE...
UH... ?
CUT!
SANA ...
THAT'S ENOUGH FOR TODAY, OKAY?
GO AND REST.
WHA?
SANA, YOU'RE OBVIOUSLY PUSHING YOURSELF TOO HARD. YOU NEED TO REST.
I'LL WORK AROUND YOU FOR A BIT.
NO, I CAN DO IT! PLEASE...
I WOULD EXPECT SUCH A WOODEN PERFORMANCE FROM A REGULAR CHILD ACTOR.
BUT I DON'T THINK OF YOU AND NAOZUMI AS CHILD ACTORS. I EXPECT BETTER.
DO YOU UNDERSTAND?
HARSH...
SANA, I'M TELLING YOU TO TAKE A BREAK.
I DON'T WANT TO SEE A SINGLE LIFELESS PERFORMANCE IN MY PRECIOUS FILM.
HE'S SO FREAKY...
MOVIES ARE MY LIFE
... YES ...
GOOD.

SCHEDULE CHANGE!
SCENE 71, PLEASE!
RIGHT AWAY!
IT'S GREAT THAT HE'S GIVING YOU A BREAK...
YOU'VE BEEN WORKING WAY TOO HARD...
びくぅっ
DON'T WORRY, SANA!
SANA... SHE'S THE STRONGEST PERSON I KNOW...
WHAT COULD HAVE POSSIBLY HAPPENED TO HER...?
ポツ
ポツ
SANA, GET SOME REST.
WE'RE ALL GOING TO HAVE TO WAIT FOR THE RAIN TO STOP ANYWAY.

The Allure of the Beauty Salon
③
(TO BE CONTINUED)
Once, I got a call from a salon right when I was on deadline, and it got me really mad.
WHERE DID YOU GET MY PHONE NUMBER, CRAZY LADY?
WHAT?
WHY?
Sometimes I ask them that (hee hee), and then I hang up on them.
The funny thing is, when I was in high school, me and my friends really wanted to go to a beauty salon. We wrote down all these names and addresses, but when we found out their prices, we would go right home in a huff. (Hee hee!)
I wonder if that's why they keep calling me...
Well, I keep on telling them where they can go—but lately, I've been thinking of giving it a try! I don't have the time right now, of course—but someday I'll be able to go. And it'll probably turn out like this:
SALON
AND WHAT WOULD YOU LIKE TODAY?
UMM... WELL... I REALLY DON'T KNOW...
ANY-THING!
JUST HELP ME, PLEASE!
I'M A WRECK!
MR. SAGAMI, HOW IS SANA?
MISS KURUMI IS TALKING TO HER.
DO YOU HAVE ANY IDEA WHAT'S GOING ON?
NO, BUT DURING THE BREAK TODAY SHE CALLED AKITO...
...AND SHE'S BEEN ACTING STRANGE EVER SINCE.
SHE CALLED ...
...AKITO...?
SANA, WHAT DID AKITO SAY TO YOU?!
WHAT?
N-NO!
TELL ME... WAS HE MEAN TO YOU? DID HE HURT YOUR FEELINGS?
'CAUSE I'LL BEAT HIM UP IF HE DID!

IT'S JUST ...
...AKITO TOLD ME THAT HE AND FUKA...
OH, YOU HAVEN'T MET FUKA! SHE'S MY BEST FRIEND...
...WELL, THEY'RE GOING OUT.
AND THE NEWS KINDA TOOK ME BY SURPRISE.
IT WAS TOO SUDDEN.
SANA...
SO THAT'S WHAT THREW YOU SO BADLY...
UM...
HANG ON! THAT'S STRANGE...
DOESN'T AKITO LIKE YOU?
NO, NOT AT ALL!
TSUYOSHI SAID SO, TOO, BUT YOU'RE BOTH WRONG!
IT'S NOT LIKE THAT!
ANYONE WOULD LIKE FUKA.
SHE'S NICE... AND GIRLIE... AND...
I DON'T BUY IT. NO WAY.
REI... HOLD ON...

LET'S CALL HIM BACK AND FIND OUT.
WE'LL GO TO THE SECRET SPOT.
"SECRET PET?"
WHAT THE—
NO, NO, SSS-POT. SPOT!
WE'LL USE THE DIRECTOR'S PHONE.
SECRET
UMM ... HANG ON!
IT'S OKAY! CUT IT OUT!
OH WAIT, I DON'T KNOW HIS NUMBER.
SANA, WHAT'S HIS NUMBER?
AAAUGH!
I SAID CUT IT OUT!!
I'LL GIVE HIM A PIECE OF MY MIND...
WHAT'S WRONG WITH YOU GUYS?
YOU GUYS GET OUT OF HERE.
SANA, I THINK IT'S TIME FOR SOME GIRL TALK.
ASAKO...
NEVER SEEN HER SO FEISTY!
④
Today It's: Let Your Friends Bury You Alive!!
PART 1 AI
Hello! I'm a comic writer who works on books for young adults. Recently, I've been helping Miho out with her greytones, because I'm really good at it.
Ⓐ Miho
★OBANA★
As I See Her...
1
ONE DAY WHEN I WAS HELPING MIHO OUT...
...OUR TALK GOT PRETTY DIRTY.
OBANA
AND I TOLD HER I HEARD THAT...
...GIRLS' COMIC WRITERS DIDN'T LIKE TALKING ABOUT THIS STUFF.
BUT... OBANA...
...LIKED IT.
SHE REALLY LIKED IT!
ARE YOU SURE YOU WRITE GIRLS' COMICS?
RIE. SHE REALLY DOESN'T LIKE TALKING ABOUT THIS STUFF.

I'M SORRY FOR BUTTING INTO THINGS HERE.
I MEAN, IT'S NOT REALLY MY BUSINESS...
NO, NO. IT'S OKAY.
REI TALKS ABOUT YOU SO MUCH, I FEEL LIKE I REALLY KNOW YOU.
SO I WANTED TO KNOW ABOUT THIS AKITO GUY, TOO.
UH-HUH ...
BUT I HAD TO ASK YOU...
...YOU REALLY LIKE HIM, DON'T YOU?
WHAT?
ME?
LIKE AKITO?
YEAH ...
ISN'T HE THE SPECIAL CALL YOU WANTED TO MAKE?
NO WAY, YOU'RE ALL WRONG !!
I JUST NEEDED TO CALL HIM...BECAUSE WHEN WE LEFT, HE TOLD ME HE NEEDED TO TALK TO ME ABOUT SOMETHING. THAT'S ALL!
I DON'T LIKE HIM THAT WAY!
REALLY?
REALLY!
I HAVE NO REASON TO LIKE A GUY LIKE HIM!
WHY NOT?

I'M LOOKING FOR SOMEONE WHO'S MATURE, AND KIND... LIKE REI!
ALSO, I LIKE MY MEN TALL, AND AKITO IS HARDLY EVEN TALLER THAN ME.
PLUS, HE'S ALWAYS LOOKING AT ME FUNNY... HE'S INCREDIBLY RUDE...
...AND HE'S A TOTAL PERVERT!
HMPF!
I ADMIT HE'S NOT ALL BAD.
BUT HE'S TOO MEAN...
...AND COLD.
BUT...
...HE CAN BE REALLY KIND AND THOUGHTFUL...
...SOMETIMES...
......
SANA,
DO YOU REALLY NEED REASONS TO FALL FOR SOMEBODY?
I MEAN...
...I COULDN'T EXPLAIN TO YOU WHAT I LIKE SO MUCH ABOUT YOU-KNOW-WHO.
I... ...I JUST KNOW THAT I DO.
I CAN'T HELP IT.
......
HMMM...
SO MISS KURUMI HAS A BOYFRIEND!
WHO COULD IT BE?
HUH? NO IDEA...
WHY'D SHE HAVE TO SAY THAT?
ききみみ

SANA'S SCHEDULE
YOU DON'T NEEDA REASON?
NOPE. AND SOMETIMES, YOU DON'T EVEN KNOW THAT YOU'VE FALLEN IN LOVE.
I SUPPOSE.
... REALLY ...?
THEN ...
...I...
...I REALLY DO LIKE HIM...

...
WHAT AN IDIOT I'VE BEEN...
MY HEART WAS BROKEN ...
...BEFORE I KNEW I WAS IN LOVE.
IF YOU EVER NEED A SHOULDER TO CRY ON, COME TO ME...
HIS WORDS CAN STILL MAKE ME FEEL BETTER...
BUT AKITO...
YOU'RE THE ONE WHO'S MAKING ME CRY...

I ALWAYS THOUGHT AKITO WAS IN LOVE WITH SANA...
...BUT HE HASN'T HEARD FROM HER IN TWO MONTHS.
I GUESS HE FOUND SOMEONE ELSE.
TWO MONTHS CAN SEEM LIKE FOREVER AT THAT AGE.
EVEN SO...
...I JUST CAN'T BELIEVE THAT SOMEONE WHO'S ALWAYS BEEN AS MATURE AND STRONG AS SANA...
...COULD BE SO WEAK IN THE FACE OF LOVE.
SANA, DON'T WORRY. WE'RE GOING TO JUST SHOOT AROUND YOU TODAY. NO PROBLEM.
GET SOME REST, OKAY?
....
SANA, SHOULD WE THINK ABOUT QUITTING?
NO! I CAN DO IT!
I'LL BE OKAY, REALLY!
ぶんっ
I HAVE TO GET BACK ON MY FEET RIGHT AWAY.
I HAVE TO STOP THINKING ABOUT AKITO!
RIGHT NOW!

THANKS EVERY-ONE! THAT'S IT FOR TONIGHT!
CRAP.
I'M NO GOOD TONIGHT, EITHER...
HE PLAYS EVERY NIGHT?
フゥ
NAOZUMI?
SANA?!
I HEARD YOU PLAYING.
WHAT WERE YOU THINKING, COMING ALL THE WAY OUT HERE? WHERE'S MR. SAGAMI?
HE'S TALKING TO MR. ONO ABOUT MY SCHEDULE.
LET'S GO BACK. SHOULDN'T YOU BE RESTING?
I'M TIRED OF SITTING IN MY ROOM ALONE.
IT GETS CREEPY...
NAOZUMI, DID YOU HEAR US TALKING LAST NIGHT AFTER YOU GUYS LEFT?
YOU WERE LISTENING, WEREN'T YOU?
UM...
YEAH, I'M SORRY.
IT'S OKAY.

I'M PATHETIC.
I TOLD YOU TO WORK HARD, AND NOW I'M THE ONE WHO'S BEING UNPROFESSIONAL!
I DON'T THINK YOU ARE...
YOU'VE DONE YOUR BEST.
......
WELL, I TRY TO DO MY BEST...
OF COURSE.
...BUT I'VE CAUSED SO MUCH TROUBLE FOR EVERYONE.
SANA ...
I DON'T KNOW WHAT TO DO.
I HAVE TO GET GOING AGAIN ...
...BUT I'M SUCH A WEAKLING.
I'M SO CONFUSED... INSIDE.
NAOZUMI? YOU'RE CRYING, TOO?
ULP!
UH...
I...

I'M THE ONE...
SNIFF
...WITH SOME-THING TO C-CR-CRY ABOUT!
SNIFF
BUT W-WHY ARE YOU CRYING?
......
flower
IT'S BECAUSE... YOU'RE CRYING.
HUUUH?
SNIFF
DON'T...
NAO...
I'M S-SO UN-HA-HA-HAPPY...

WHAT? NAO...
SANA...
I'VE...
...ALWAYS LOVED YOU.

I'LL BE HERE FOR YOU.
SO, SANA...
PLEASE DON'T CRY!
NAOZUMI...

MR. SAGAMI. WE CAN STILL WORK AROUND SANA TOMORROW...
...BUT NOT MORE THAN ANOTHER DAY OR TWO AFTER THAT.
SHE'S IN MOST OF THE SCENES WE HAVE LEFT.
NO PROBLEM. ONE MORE DAY OF REST IS ALL SHE NEEDS, I'M SURE.
I HOPE!
BUT... WHAT IF SHE DOESN'T...
うーむ…
I JUST CAN'T SEEM TO SNAP HER OUT OF THIS.
SHE CAN'T SEEM TO GET BETTER ON HER OWN, AND I CAN'T DO ANYTHING...
WAIT... I KNOW...
I'LL CALL HER!
SHE'S OUR ONLY HOPE!
MR. ONO!
QUICK, LET ME BORROW YOUR EMERGENCY CELL PHONE!
ALL RIGHT, BUT YOU'RE GONNA OWE ME FOR THE CALL...
WHAT A CHEAP-SKATE!
THE NEXT DAY...
バラララ
WOW!
A HELICOP-TER!
WHAT'S IT DOING UP HERE?
バラララ
I THINK IT'S HEADING THIS WAY.
UNLESS I'M CRAZY...
NO, HERE IT COMES!
バラララ
ARE THEY CRASH LANDING?
WHAT ARE YOU DOING?
AAAAAGH!

パカ…
....
プルプルプル
おおっ!?
THANK YOU FOR TAKING CARE OF MY DAUGHTER.
プルプル
プル
I HEARD SHE WAS HAVING SOME TROUBLE, SO I FLEW RIGHT OVER.
HELLO.
MISS KURATA... YOUR DEAD-LINE...
IT'S MARIKO KURATA! LOOK AT HER HAIR!
MISS KURATA...
...AND HER EDITOR!
YOU CERTAIN-LY DID FLY RIGHT OVER...
MISS KURATA! MA'AM! THANKS FOR COMING RIGHT AWAY!
プルプルプル
AH!
MR. SAGAMI!
THANKS FOR CALLING ME.
A HELICOPTER?
WHERE DID SHE GET IT?
コンコンッ
SANA! SOMEONE'S HERE TO SEE YOU!
REI?
I DON'T WANNA SEE ANYONE...
ギイ..

HELLO.
MO...
MOMMY!
がばっ
COME HERE, SANA.
MOM!
MOM!
MR. SAGAMI TOLD ME WHAT HAP-PENED.
MOM...
HOW IS YOUR LEG?
IT'S STILL ACHY...BUT I'LL BE FINE.
GOOD...
MOM... I CAN'T WORK ANY MORE! I HAVE NO FOCUS! I CAN'T DO IT!
THEY HAD TO RE-ARRANGE THE WHOLE SHOOTING SCHEDULE AROUND ME...
I'M CAUSING SO MANY PROBLEMS FOR EVERY-ONE! I'VE BECOME A "PROBLEM CHILD"!
I SEE...
AND... AKITO...
SNIFF
I HEARD.
I CAN'T GET HIM OUT OF MY HAIR...
THAT'S "YOUR MIND."
...AND IF I CAN'T, I WON'T BE ABLE TO WORK ANYMORE...
AND NAOZUMI TOLD ME THAT HE LOVES ME...
...AND I DON'T KNOW WHAT TO DO!

DON'T BE SUCH A BABY!
AAUGH!
MOM!
HOW CAN YOU TREAT A BROKEN HEART THIS WAY?
YOU CAN'T JUST FORGET ABOUT YOUR TROUBLES, SANA.
IF SOMETHING'S BOTHERING YOU, THEN YOU NEED TO THINK ABOUT IT AND WORK IT OUT!
BUT I HAVE TO FORGET, SO I CAN WORK.
ぴこんっ
ALL RIGHT NOW, LET'S TRY THIS!
GET OVER HERE.
WHEN I AM REALLY UPSET ABOUT SOMETHING, I WRITE IT DOWN ON PAPER, IN A "WORRY BOOK."
MAYBE IT'LL WORK FOR YOU...
YOU WRITE IT DOWN?
I SHOULD HAVE GUESSED!
HEY, WHERE ARE WE?
I'M ON A DEADLINE, SO I NEED TO GET SOME WORK DONE.
YOU SIT HERE AND WORRY AS MUCH AS YOU NEED TO.
SANA, YOU'RE STRONG ENOUGH TO TURN YOUR TROUBLES INTO SOMETHING POSITIVE.
NO, I'M NOT!
SNIFF
YES, YOU ARE...
...BECAUSE YOU'RE MY DAUGHTER!
YOU'RE JUST FEELING LOW RIGHT NOW.

Akito
Me
SCRITCH
SOME DAY, YOU'LL LOOK BACK AND YOU WON'T BELIEVE THIS UPSET YOU SO MUCH!
BUT IT DOES UPSET ME...
JUST START WRITING!
love
......
AAAAUGH!
EXPRESS YOURSELF ON PAPER, NOT OUT LOUD!!! YOU'RE SO NOISY!
Naozumi
....
Akito
Fuka
dating

HMM....
すー
Akito
Fuka
love met
friends
strangers
friends
Naozumi
Me
Maro
MAYBE IT'S NOT AS BAD AS I THOUGHT...
ピチチチ...
ぱか
WIDE AWAKE
HUH?
プー
パー

WELL, I'M NO GOOD THIS MORNING.
EVERY MORNING, TOO!
NAOZUMI! GOOD MORNING!
AAH! SHE SURPRISED ME!
MORNING, SANA.
ISN'T IT PRETTY OUT?
PRETTY AS A PICTURE!
ひゃははっ
......
WOW... FEELING BETTER, HUH?
YUP!
I LET MYSELF REALLY WORRY FOR A WHILE LIKE MOM TOLD ME TO... AND WHEN I WOKE UP, I FELT ALL BETTER!
HA HA!
SIMPLE, HUH?
YOU SEE...
I REALIZED, THINGS AREN'T REALLY ALL THAT BAD RIGHT NOW.
I'VE ALSO LEARNED THAT I DON'T NEED TO WORRY ABOUT HAVING A REASON TO LIKE SOMEONE.
AND THAT IT'S OKAY TO FEEL HOWEVER I NEED TO FEEL...

IT'S OKAY TO KEEP ON FEELING THIS WAY...
...EVEN IF HE DOESN'T FEEL THE SAME.
......
BUT ...
...WON'T THAT BE TOUGH ON YOU?
MAYBE...
BUT I'M GOING TO TRY MY BEST.
I SEE.
ピチチ
UM...
NAOZUMI...
WHEN YOU TOLD ME THAT YOU LOVED ME...
...IT REALLY MADE ME FEEL BETTER.
THANK YOU.

TOO BLUNT
BUT, I'VE REALIZED I CAN ONLY GO OUT WITH SOMEONE I REALLY FEEL IN LOVE WITH. SORRY...
SANA ...
...IT'S ALL RIGHT.
I'LL FOLLOW YOUR EXAMPLE ...
...AND I WON'T EXPECT YOU TO FEEL THE SAME WAY, EITHER.
WELL... LET'S GET GOING, OKAY?
TODAY'S MY BIG COMEBACK!
WHAT? CAN YOU REALLY DO IT?
SURE!
I'VE HAD 3 DAYS OFF...
SANA!
AGH!
ARE YOU OKAY?

WANT ME TO CARRY YOU?
NO, NO, I'M FINE.
SEE?
I CAN DO IT MYSELF.
YOU LOOK MUCH BETTER, SANA.
I'M FEELING SO MUCH BETTER! THANKS A LOT, MOM! ♡
THANKS, MOM! ♡
DO YOUR BEST, NOW.
I WILL!
SHOOTING ON LOCATION IS ALMOST OVER. I'M GOING TO DO MY BEST TO MAKE UP FOR ALL THE TROUBLE I'VE CAUSED!
YOU DO YOUR BEST, TOO, MOM!

MY LEG STILL HURTS... BUT AFTER THREE DAYS OF RESTING IT, I THINK IT'LL BE OKAY.
I'M SO LUCKY!
I'M FEELIN' GREAT!
SANA, YOU LOOK FINE! ARE YOU REALLY OKAY?
NOW COMES THE BIG FINALE...
MAKO COMES OUT OF THE BURNING MANSION!
IT'S A LITTLE DANGEROUS...
ALL THE TREES NEARBY HAVE BEEN CHOPPED DOWN.
OKAY NOW, LET'S FOLLOW THE PLAN! I DON'T WANT ANY MISTAKES!
QUIET, EVERYONE!!
SANA, AS SOON AS YOU HEAR THIS ALARM SOUND, COME OUT.
I'LL SET IT OFF AS SOON AS THE FIRE STARTS TO SPREAD.
FINAL CHECK
WE'RE GOING TO DO OUR BEST TO KEEP THE SMOKE AND FIRE AWAY FROM THE MAIN ENTRANCE, BUT IT'S STILL GOING TO GET HOT IN THERE.
SO BE CAREFUL!
GOT IT!
I'LL BE FINE!
WHEN YOUR MIND IS CLEARED OUT, EVEN FIRE IS NO SWEAT!
NO SWEAT, NO SWEAT.
WELL, AT LEAST SHE'S BACK TO NORMAL...
WIPE
SHE MEANS:
IF YOUR MIND IS FREE AND CLEAR, EVEN FIRE WILL FEEL COOL.
HUH?
UH, IT'S OKAY IF YOU SWEAT... WE'LL JUST CLEAN IT UP IN THE FINAL PRINT.
OKAY! THEN I'LL SWEAT MY HEART OUT!
BRING IT ON! BRING IT ON!

GOOD LUCK, EVERYONE!
BE CARE-FUL!
ONCE THEY BURN THIS PLACE DOWN, THEY CAN'T USE IT AGAIN.
HERE'S WHERE I WAIT.
WOW, I CAN HARDLY SIT DOWN...
AND YOU RUN TO GRAB MAKO WHEN SHE COMES OUT.
RIGHT.
SO I HAVE TO BE PER-FECT.
OKAY!
C'MON!
ALL RIGHT! SCENE 92!
EVERY-BODY BE CARE-FUL!
OKAY!
REMEMBER, WE ONLY HAVE ONE CHANCE AT THIS!
LIGHT IT UP!
OKAY!
I'M READY!
STEADY!

......
WOW... IT'S REALLY HOT.
I DIDN'T THINK IT WOULD BE LIKE THIS...
IS THIS PART OF THE HOUSE REALLY SAFE?
THIS IS WAY HOTTER THAN I THOUGHT...
THE SIGNAL!!
HERE I COME!
!?

WHY ISN'T SHE OUT YET?
GIVE THE SIGNAL AGAIN!
!?
AH...MY LEG...
I HURT IT AGAIN ...
I CAN'T MOVE!!
SANA...?
SANA!

AAAH!!!
IT'S GETTING SO HOT!
SOME-THING'S GONE WRONG!
STOP THE CAMERAS AND PUT THE FIRE OUT!
NO!

I SAID, WE ONLY HAVE ONE CHANCE AT THIS!
WHAT ARE YOU TALKING ABOUT? SANA...
THIS IS GOING TO BE PERFECT! THESE FLAMES ARE EXACTLY WHAT I WANTED! SO BE QUIET!
YOU SICK—
DON'T WORRY! THE ENTRANCE IS REINFORCED AND FLAME-PROOFED. SHE'LL BE FINE!
HOW CAN YOU BE SURE?!
KEEP FILMING!! AND SIGNAL AGAIN!
I CAN'T STAND UP! WHAT AM I GOING TO DO?
OOF ...
OH, NO...
ARGH
I'M GONNA DIE...
THEY SAID THERE WOULDN'T BE ANY SMOKE IN HERE!
LIARS!
THERE'S TOO MUCH SMOKE! I CAN'T BREATHE!
THIS IS REALLY HAPPENING!
UGGGH.
AM I DYING?

DYING ...?
ゴ
バキ
IF I DIE HERE...
パ4
パ4
...I WON'T SEE FUKA AND AKITO AND KNOW WHAT HAPPENED...
がく
がく
....
ずる
ゴホ
パ4
パ4

I CAN'T WAIT!! GO IN AFTER HER!
NO!
IT'LL BE SAFE FOR THREE MORE MINUTES!
YOU'RE WRONG!
SANA HAS A BROKEN LEG!
SHE MIGHT NOT BE ABLE TO WALK! STOP FILMING!
WHAT? BROKEN?
I HAD NO IDEA!
NO! WE'RE NOT STOPPING!
DON'T YOU REALIZE HER LIFE MAY BE IN DANGER?!
IF ANYTHING HAPPENS TO SANA, I'M WILLING TO DIE WITH HER!
BUT THIS MOVIE WILL BE OUR LEGACY!!
MOVIES ARE MY LIFE
ARE YOU CRAZY?!?!
ぎゅ

THAT'S IT!
だっ
MR. SAGAMI?
SOME-BODY STOP HIM!
WAIT, MR. SAGAMI!
THEY CAN'T DO THIS AGAIN! IF THE FILM IS RUINED, NO ONE'S GOING TO REGRET IT MORE THAN SANA!
I THINK SHE'D PUT HER LIFE ON THE LINE FOR THE FILM!
NAO-ZUMI!
PLEASE, JUST GIVE HER A FEW MORE MINUTES!
SANA... PLEASE HURRY...
DON'T LET ALL YOUR WORK GO TO WASTE!

I'M SO... TIRED...
EVERYONE... GOODBYE.
ゴオ…
パチ
パチ
SANA IS GOING TO THE NEXT WORLD AHEAD OF YOU...
パチ
パチ
ひらっ…
ぴと…
HUH?
じゅう…
YEEEOWCH!!
ふんがーっ
がばっ

AH! THAT WAS HOT!
OWIE!
ふーふーっ
はっ...
NOW LOOK WHAT I'VE DONE.
HUH?!
ゴホッ
I...
WHAT AM I DOING?
DID I LET THE PAIN...
...MAKE ME WEAK?
ハァ
I HAVE TO GET OUT OF HERE!
ズキ
ズキ
がし
がし
がし
がくんっ
OOF...

MR. ONO! THIS ISN'T LOOKING VERY GOOD...
I'M GOING TO HAVE THEM PUT OUT THE FIRE, OKAY?
SANA!
COME ON, SANA!
WHAT ARE YOU DOING IN THERE? HURRY UP!
SANA!
...NAOZUMI ?
SNAP OUT OF IT!

......
すぅ…
MAKO'S COMING!
I HEARD HER!
HUH?
YOU HEARD SANA?
SHE'S COM-ING!
CAMERA!
READY!
SANA!
ハァ
ハァ
ゴホッ
ハァッ
がく
がく
がく
がく
UGH...
I... CAN'T ...
ズキッ

ハア
PANT!
ゴホッ
がく
がく
ハア
I'M NOT AS STRONG...
...AS EVERYONE THINKS...
...I AM.
ゴオ…
DO YOUR BEST!
DO YOUR BEST!
DO YOUR BEST!
...BUT ...
...BREATHE...

ゴオ
I'M STILL GOING TO DO MY BEST!

キ
THERE SHE IS!
SHH!
ゴ
ゴオ
ドドオッ
ゴ

HOLY CRAP!
MAKO—!!
MAKO !!
WH... WHAT HAPPENED ?
WHERE ARE MY BROTHERS?
THEY'RE INSIDE...
ALL BURNED...
HEHEHEH...
WHAT ?!
NO... MAKO ...
DID YOU DO THIS?!
MAKO ?!
HE HE HEH.

YES, I TOOK THEIR LIVES ...
... BECAUSE I LOVE THEM.
AND ... ME?
I DIDN'T TAKE YOU...
... BECAUSE I LOVE YOU.
LIVE... FOR ME...
CUT!
GREAT!!

OKAY! GREAT!
GET THE FIRE OUT!
YOU KIDS, GET OVER HERE!
HURRY!
GREAT?
SANA!
...!?
AGH!
NAOZUMI... DID I GET MY LINES RIGHT?
YOU WERE PERFECT!
C'MON!
SANA!
PUT OUT THE FIRE!

BACK UP!
WE NEED A DOCTOR!
COMING!
NAO!
キャ
GANGWAY! NAOZUMI IS HURT!
バタタタ
MR. ONO! THE LOCALS ARE COMPLAINING ABOUT THE FIRE!
WE'RE MAKING MOVIES! WHO'S AFRAID OF A FEW COM-PLAINTS?
GET SANA THE OXY-GEN!
SANA, WHAT HAPPENED TO YOU IN THERE?
I WASN'T CAREFUL.
I SAT DOWN TO WAIT, AND WHEN I TRIED TO GET UP, I FELT A SHARP PAIN...
SANA! ARE YOU ALL RIGHT?
Y... YES.
I CAN'T BELIEVE YOU DID THIS WITH A BROKEN LEG!
YEAH... WHERE'S MR. ONO?

WOOOW...
MR. ONO! IT'S AMAZING!
IT'S EXACTLY HOW YOU WANTED IT TO LOOK!
CHECK IT OUT!
MR. ONO!
MR. ONO!
HOW WAS IT?

......
ぐっ
ほっ
SANA! YOU WERE GREAT!
GOOD JOB!
YOU WERE AMAZING!
WANT TO TAKE A QUICK LOOK BEFORE THE DOCTOR SEES YOU?
パチ
WAY TO GO, SANA!
YOU HAD US SCARED!
ボケー

……
ニヤ…
LOOK AT THAT!
HMPF!
ぱち ぱち
SANA!!
パチ
SANA... YOU REALLY WERE GREAT ...
BUT I THINK I LOST A FEW YEARS OF MY LIFE THERE...
……
HEH.
AND SO...
...THE LOCATION SHOOT FINALLY ENDED.
プスス…
DON'T PLAY WITH MATCHES ...
HUH?
SANA! HANG ON!
GET THE DOC-TOR!
……
くてん

CONGRATULATIONS, EVERYONE! OUR LOCATION SHOOT IS A WRAP!
THANK YOU FOR ALL YOUR HARD WORK! WE'LL SEE YOU ALL ON THE SET BACK IN TOKYO!
おつかれ
YOUR LEG BROKE AGAIN, SANA?
YEAH, LOOKS LIKE I PUT PRESSURE ON THE FRACTURE WHEN I JUMPED UP LIKE THAT.
I JUST CAN'T BELIEVE YOU WERE WORKING WITH A BROKEN LEG...
YOU SEEMED OKAY!
NAOZUMI, I HEARD YOU GOT BURNED...
ARE YOU OKAY?
I'M FINE...
...BUT DON'T TOUCH!
I MEAN IT.
YOU TWO WERE GREAT.
MR. ONO!
THANK YOU... MY FILM IS GOING TO BE TERRIFIC.
I CAN'T WAIT TO SEE IT!
I'M SORRY I PUSHED YOU SO HARD.
NO PROBLEM! I HAVE INSURANCE...
SANA, THAT'S NOT WHAT HE MEANS...
WAHAHAHAH!
MR. ONO, HOW DID YOU GET THAT SCAR? WAS IT ON A SET?
YEAH. I WAS WORKING THE CAMERA WHEN THE CRANE SUDDENLY BROKE...
ゴツン
がくんっ
ブシュ
AH HA HA HA
MICKEY, YOU'RE SO GOOFY...
"MICKEY?"
IT'S "MIKIO," AND YOU SHOULD SAY "MR. ONO"...
MAN...

⑤
Today It's:
Let Your Friends Bury You Alive!!
PART 2
RIE
Miho and I had been friends for a long time before I started helping her out on the Kodocha junior high school saga! I'm the one drawing the backgrounds. You know, without people like me, the story couldn't go on!
Miho Obana!
As I see her...
by RIE Seki
SOME-TIMES WHEN WE'RE WORK-ING AND SHE NEEDS TO FOCUS...
...MIHO WILL DRAW AN EYE AND TAPE IT TO HER FORE-HEAD.
FOCUS!
AMAZING! YOU'RE STILL AWAKE!
SHE SAYS IT CAN HELP HER STAY UP AND WORK.
...YOU SURE GOT A LOT DONE THERE...
SHH...
OBANA, A WOMAN OF MYSTERY!!
MR. ONO HAS NO SENSE OF HUMOR...
WHISPER, WHISPER
EVERY-THING TURNED OUT ALL RIGHT BUT...
I CAN'T STAND HIM.
WELL, MOVIES REALLY ARE HIS LIFE.
I THINK HE'S GREAT.
WHEN YOU SEE THE RESULT, YOU'LL AGREE WITH HIM.
SANA, THOSE GIRLS WANT TO TALK TO YOU.
I THINK THEY WANT TO APOLO-GIZE...
WILL YOU TALK TO THEM?
......
SURE, I'LL LET THEM SAY THEY'RE SORRY...
HELLO!
I HEAR YOU WANT TO TALK TO ME.

WELL ...
YES?
WE'LL NEVER LIKE YOU...
...BUT WE HAVE TO ADMIT, YOU WORK HARD...
SO, WE'RE SORRY ABOUT YOUR LEG.
OH, PUH-LEAZE ...
THAT'S HOW THEY SAY "SORRY"?
WELL, THERE'S SOMEONE I REALLY LIKE, TOO!
AHEM.
BUT I JUST FIGURED IT OUT, SO IT'S STILL PRETTY EMBARRASSING!
たはーっ
てね
......
LOOK...
YOU ALL REALLY LIKE NAOZUMI, RIGHT?

BUT HE'S GOING OUT WITH MY FRIEND...
...SO I THINK I CAN UNDERSTAND HOW YOU FEEL.
I JUST WANTED YOU...
...TO KNOW THAT.
ROTTEN BRATS!
GETTING ANGRY..
I'M SORRY!
YEAH, YEAH.
NO PROBLEM.
LATER!
OH! AND BE SURE TO SEE THE MOVIE!
BYE-BYE!
WE'LL SEE IT...
...FOR NAOZUMI.
I THINK THEY'RE GOING TO END UP BEING FANS OF SANA...

HEY, SANA.
HM?
YOU WERE GREAT!
YOU, TOO!
SEE YOU IN TOKYO?
YUP!
FINALLY...
...WE'RE GOING HOME!
GOOD-BYE, MOUNTAIN!
WE GOT BACK IN THE MIDDLE OF SUMMER VACATION.
カーッ
I HAD TO STAY IN THE HOSPITAL UNTIL MY LEG GOT BETTER.
UGH, IT'S SO HOT!
IT WAS SO MUCH NICER IN THE MOUNTAINS...
I FEEL SO LAZY.
バタ バタ バタ バタ
氷
SO? WHAT ARE YOU GOING TO DO NEXT?
DIDN'T WE HAVE THIS TALK...?

⑥
Today It's: Let Your Friends Bury You Alive!!
PART 3 AI AGAIN
Ⓐ Miho OBANA
As seen by Ai 2
In '96, when I met up with Obana for coffee....
COFFEE
...she was all dressed up.
YO.
AND NEXT TO THAT...
...SUNGLASSES!
THERE WAS COFFEE...
...BY HER HAND
YO.
キリッ
SHE LOOKED LIKE...
...HIROSHI TACHI!*
~DANDY~
I THOUGHT MAYBE SHE WAS TRYING TO SEDUCE ME...
SHE WAS SUCH A DANDY! I GOT EXCITED AND MY NOSE STARTED TO BLEED!
...BUT LATER I FOUND OUT THAT SHE ONLY WORE SUNGLASSES BECAUSE HER EYES ARE SO SENSITIVE TO SUNLIGHT...
* HIROSHI TACHI: A HEARTTHROB ACTOR AND SINGER.
WHEN I WAS BETTER, WE WENT TO WORK AGAIN, THIS TIME ON A SET.
WOW! IT'S JUST LIKE THE MANSION! ♡
AND AFTER A LOT MORE HARD WORK...
SANA... HAVE YOU TALKED TO ANYONE SINCE YOU GOT BACK?
NO, NOT YET...
I DON'T THINK ANYONE KNOWS I'M HOME.
OH...
GOOD LUCK.
YOU, TOO.
...

WE LEFT FOR LOCATION IN MID-MAY...
...SO IT'S BEEN FOUR MONTHS SINCE I'VE SEEN EVERYONE.
ドキ
ドキ
I'M SO NERVOUS!
ドキ
SANA'S FIRST SUMMER UNIFORM
WILL I BE ABLE TO ACT LIKE EVERYTHING'S COOL?
ドキドキドキ
I'LL BE OKAY...
I'VE HAD TIME TO GET READY FOR THIS...
OKAY, OKAY!
キー!
YIKES! 2ND PERIOD IS OVER!
REALLY LATE
たたっ
ヘーイ
HEY! IT'S SANA!
LONG TIME, NO SEE! ♡
ざわ
ARE YOU ALL DONE WITH THAT MOVIE?
YUP! ALL DONE!
WELCOME BACK!
HEY! SANA'S BACK!

OH...
たたっ
......
YO! FUKA!
HEY, GIRL! YOU'RE BACK!
がしっ
とな
スタスタ
スタスタ

キャー
キャー
IT'S BEEN AGES! WHEN DID YOU GET BACK?
UH, ABOUT THE MIDDLE OF SUMMER VACA-TION.
WHAT? WHY DIDN'T YOU CALL?
WHEW...
WELL, THERE WAS A LOT GOING ON...
IT'S LIKE I NEVER LEFT!
あはは
HEY! HEY!
SANA'S BACK!
WHAT?
1-1
IT'S TRUE! THERE SHE IS!
バタバタバタ
HI!!
TSUYOSHI! AYA!
SANA, IT SEEMS LIKE FOR-EVER!
I KNOW...
HOW ARE YOU?
WE ALL MISSED YOU...
YEAH, ME, TOO...
ドキ
あ
AKITO...
BE COOL, BE COOL...
ドキ
ドキ
HEY, AKITO!
LOOK, IT'S SANA!

AKITO?!
YO...
STILL ALIVE, HUH?
!?!?
WHA-?
TY-PICAL AKITO...
WHAT THE-?
HEY, SANA SEEMS LIKE SHE'S IN SHOCK...
WELL, OF COURSE SHE IS! NOT EVERYONE GROWS TWO INCHES IN FOUR MONTHS!
TWO INCHES... IN FOUR MONTHS...?!
SOME GROWTH SPURT, HUH? I'LL BET HIS JOINTS CREAK AT NIGHT.
THEY'RE ACHY ALL THE TIME...
DON'T BE SUCH AN OLD MAN...
...OR BABY...
DO THEY?
WOW, EVEN HIS VOICE IS DIFFERENT!

WOW, THAT'S ALMOST SCARY ...
WHAT DID YOU BRING ME?
WHAT?!
NOTHING! THERE WASN'T ANYTHING UP THERE AT ALL!
LIKE I'D BRING YOU A SOU-VENIR ...
HMPF.
MEANIE.
キーンコーン
WHAT'S WITH HIM?
THE BELL!
WHAT'S NEXT?
ENG-LISH!
FUKA!
HM?
ド
キ
BE RIGHT BACK! GOTTA STOP BY THE BATHROOM!
GO TO THE BATHROOM!
WE HEARD YOU THE FIRST TIME, SANA...
OKAY ...
GIVE ME YOUR DIC-TIONARY.
THE ENGLISH ONE.
WHAT? AGAIN?
CAN'T YOU EVER BRING YOUR OWN?
BUT IT'S HEAVY ...
OH, PLEASE!!
ドキ ドキ
ドキ
ドキ

SOMEHOW ...
カラ…
SC-
SCHOOL IS SO MUCH HARDER THAN WORK!
Conserve Water

I NEVER THOUGHT JUST GOING TO SCHOOL COULD BE SO DIFFICULT.
I WAS WRONG... IT'S NOTHING LIKE BEFORE...
MY HEART'S POUNDING...
I'M TENSE...
GOOD, HE'S GONE.
BUT I CAN DO IT. I'LL DO MY BEST.
I KNOW I CAN, BECAUSE...
I'M THE WOMAN WHO AMAZED EVEN THE CIRCUS LIONS WITH HER DARING ESCAPE FROM THE FIRE!
A WOMAN WHO CAN STAND UP TO FIRE CAN STAND UP TO ANYTHING!
BWA HA HA HA HA!
HER HAIR IS SINGED!
EVEN PRINCESS TENKO* WOULD BE AMAZED BY MY DARING!
HA HA HA!
MROWR?
* REMEMBER PRINCESS TENKO THE MAGICIAN? SHE HAD HER OWN CARTOON HERE A WHILE BACK!
OKAY!
TO THE CLASSROOM!
YEE HAW!
......

CLASS 8'S HOME-ROOM TEACHER, MR. SUZUKI.
WELL, HELLO, MISS KURATA. HAVEN'T SEEN YOU FOR A WHILE...
HELLO! IT HAS BEEN A WHILE!
WELL, YOU DO YOUR BEST TO CATCH UP, ALL RIGHT?
......
HEARING NO EVIL
キーン
コーン...
SANA, I TOOK EXTRA NOTES FOR YOU.
WHAT?!

WOW! FROM EVERY CLASS? EVERYTHING?
WELL, JUST THE IMPORTANT STUFF...
...SO YOU CAN CATCH UP QUICK.
NOTE BOOK
数学
これは覚えなあかん!
しんせつ（笑）
HA HA!!
AFTER ALL, IF THERE'S ANYTHING I DON'T GET, THEN AN IGNORAMUS LIKE YOU AIN'T GONNA GET IT.
TO BE BLUNT...
I DIDN'T EVEN ASK HER TO DO THIS...
ぢ〜ん。
I'M NOT CRYING BECAUSE I'M SAD...
IT'S 'CAUSE I'M SO HAPPY...
SURE...
WELL, I'M GLAD YOU'RE HAPPY!
C'MON, GIRL, NOW PAY UP!
EH...
YOU DRIVE A HARD BARGAIN!
SHE'S REALLY SHARP!
8 PAGES, SO GIMME EIGHT BUCKS.
FUKA!
COME HERE!
WHAT?
I NEED HELP...
WOW, THESE NOTES ARE AMAZING!
SANA, FUKA'S REALLY SMART, DID YOU KNOW?
SHE WAS NINTH IN OUR CLASS!
I WANT THEM...
CAN I COPY THEM?
REALLY?
AND NEXT YEAR, SHE'LL BE CLASS REPRESENTATIVE!
FUKA?

AND SHE'S GREAT AT GYM-NASTICS!
SHE DID REALLY WELL AT THE REGIONAL MEET.
THE PRINCIPAL GAVE HER AN AWARD AT THE ASSEMBLY.
GOOD JOB, YOUNG LADY!
HO HO!!
THANKS.
LOOK THIS WAY, FUKA!
WOW!
FUKA'S DOING SO WELL HERE... I'M AMAZED!
WHY AM I SUCH A LOSER?
PLUS, SHE'S GOT A PRETTY COOL BOYFRIEND.
HE'S FROM CLASS 1.
I'M TOTALLY JEALOUS!
COOL? AKITO?
YEAH ...
HMM...
Cafeteria
OH, THERE'S TSUYOSHI AND EVERY-ONE.
LET'S GO SIT DOWN!

NO... UH, HERE'S FINE. TOO MANY PEOPLE OVER THERE.
HUH?
UM... FUKA.
YEAH?
YOU'RE GOING OUT WITH AKITO NOW?
OH... SOME-ONE TOLD YOU?
YEAH.
I WAS SURPRISED!
WHAT MADE YOU WANNA GO OUT WITH HIM?
WELL, WHY NOT?
OH! YOU GOTTA SHOW UP FOR GYMNAS-TICS AT LEAST ONCE!!
WHAT ABOUT TODAY?
AH... SURE, I GUESS...
FUKA...

⑦

Hello, I'm back!

So how did you like the "Let Your Friends Bury You Alive!" segments? I thought it would be fun to have some of my friends share with you what they think of me. I guess I'm a pretty strange woman! (Hee-hee!) I hope you enjoy all the little bonus comics and stuff!

Well, back to Kodocha. Sana has finally awakened to love! Hee-hee! Usually, when I write serious material, I try to lighten it up a little. But I guess I can't really do that with something as serious as true love. (Especially when I get the impression that what's going on between Sana and Akito is what's really most important to Kodocha's readers, and that they're really affected by it...) So when I'm writing about things like unrequited love, I always think, "I shouldn't poke fun at this, it's serious!" But actually, now that I think about it... When I read through this volume over again, I think I'm still kinda poking fun! (Hee-hee!) Don't worry, I'll be taking it more seriously starting in volume 7. When I first started volume 7, the first draft had a lot of jokes in it. A lot! But when I went to re-read it, I decided I wanted to make things much more serious, so I totally rewrote it. I was pretty hesitant about this at first... But now I'm glad I did it!

IT'S NO BIGGIE.
I'VE BEEN DOIN' IT FOR YOU.
THANKS
YOU KNOW, FUKA AND I GET ALONG REALLY WELL.
I THINK WE'RE REALLY GOOD FRIENDS BUT...
WILL MR. SUZUKI PLEASE REPORT TO THE PRINCIPAL'S OFFICE?
THE PRINCIPAL IS WAITING.
WE ACTUALLY HAVEN'T EVEN SPENT A MONTH TOGETHER...
...SO IT'S ONLY NATURAL THAT THERE'D BE THINGS I DON'T GET ABOUT HER YET.
PLEASE HURRY, OR THE PRINCIPAL WILL GET MAD!
MR. SUZUKI...
I WONDER WHEN SHE'S GONNA BRING AKITO UP...
バタ バタ バタ
AA-AAH!
!?
M-MISTER SUZUKI?
YOU SHOULDN'T RUN IN THE HALLS!
SHE SHOULDN'T BE PLAYING AROUND WITH THE FLOWER-POTS.
SORRY, SANA!
I WAS IN A RUSH.
OOOH...
AH, IT'S NOT BROKEN!
SORRY!
HEY, YOU!
OVER THERE!
GO HELP SANA CLEAN UP, PLEASE.
I GOTTA GO...
SURE...

バコ
SORRY!
バタバタ
ゴトン
ドキドキドキ
UH... NOW WHAT?!
ふき
WHAT WERE YOU DOING?
UH, I'M IN CHARGE OF FLOWERS.
ポト
....HUH... ....
YOUR TEACHER SEEMS NICE.
WHAT? AH... UH, YEAH, I THINK SO...
MY HOME-ROOM TEACHER SUCKS.
YOU GOT MR. SENSEKI, RIGHT? THE SCIENCE TEACHER.
YEAH, HE'S CREEPY.
ふき
ふき
ふき

THIS IS SO SURREAL ...
...AKITO OBEYING A TEACHER? AND CLEANING THE FLOOR?
HAS HE CHANGED INSIDE, TOO?
SO, TWO INCHES IN FOUR MONTHS... YOU'RE GOING TO END UP LIKE GIANT BABA IF YOU DON'T WATCH OUT...*
......
AND SO WHAT IF I DO?
*THE FAMOUS WRESTLER GIANT BABA WAS 6'10"!!
WELL, EVERYTHING SEEMS NORMAL BETWEEN US.
SQUEEZE
YOU'RE DOING THAT ALL WRONG!
HUH?
THIS IS HOW YOU WRING A CLOTH OUT.
LOOK...
UMM... LIKE THIS?
WHAT'S WITH HIM...
THAT'S IT!
I'M A WRINGING PRO...
HEY, AKITO, HOW'S KARATE BEEN GOING?
KARATE ...?
WELL, I'M FINALLY GETTING TO DO A LOT OF NEW THINGS...

...SO IT'S STARTING TO BE FUN.
COOL!
SANA...
WHEN DID YOU GET A BRA?
I CAN SEE IT!
AGH! HE HASN'T CHANGED A BIT!
PERVERT!
HA! MY DEFENSE ...
...ISN'T GOOD ENOUGH!
SWING

I HAD TWO...
.....
ACK!
びたっ
ぶん
COULD HE REALLY SEE MY BRA?
IT DOES HAVE A RED PATTERN...
THAT'S WHY HE COULD SEE IT!
I GUESS I BETTER JUST WEAR WHITE ONES.
HEY! YOU CAN'T JUST THROW RAGS AT PEOPLE...!
スタ スタ
....
BEING A WOMAN IS ROUGH!
HEY, GIRL.
HUH?
NOW WHAT?!
I'M FINISHED WITH THIS.
COULD YOU GIVE THIS TO FUKA?
UM, SURE...
......?
スタ スタ
HEY!
HOLD IT RIGHT THERE!

WHAT DID YOU SAY TO ME?
......
UH, "GIVE THIS BACK..."
NO, BEFORE!
...... "HEY, GIRL"?
HOW DARE YOU!
おぅおぅっ
HUH?
HOW DARE YOU BE SO CASUAL WITH ME!
WHAT'S THE BIG DEAL?
I SHOULD HAVE SAID, "SAM".
LAUGHING AT A MEMORY
YOU CAN'T JUST CALL ME "GIRL" LIKE THAT!
ぷ
OH... I SEE...
I GUESS PEOPLE DO PICK UP ON HOW THE PEOPLE THEY HANG AROUND WITH TALK...
I GUESS...
FUKA ALWAYS SAYS THAT TO YOU, AND I MUST HAVE COPIED HER...
!!
NEXT, YOU'LL PROBABLY BE PICKING UP HER ACCENT!

WELL, I'M NOT AROUND FUKA THAT MUCH...
WHAT-EVER!!
DON'T TALK TO ME THAT WAY AGAIN!
AND DON'T MAKE ME TELL YOU TWICE...
GOT IT?
WAS THAT REALLY SUCH A BIG DEAL?
プイッ
スタ
スタ
I AM SO MAD!
I AM SO TOTALLY MAD AT HIM!
ドスドスドス
I DON'T EVEN KNOW WHY!!
BUT I'M ANGRY...
I PROBABLY LOOKED LIKE A TOTAL IDIOT, GETTING SO MAD...
ドスドスドス
WELL, I AM AN IDIOT...
バン
SANA, WHEN YOU FEEL LIKE THINGS ARE AT THEIR WORST, TRY TO ENJOY YOURSELF THE MOST.
SHE'S RIGHT!
I NEED TO RELAX...
Yes, mom!
THAT'S IT!

I CAN ENJOY MYSELF EVEN IF THEY ARE GOING OUT!
YEAH !!
JUST YOU WATCH ME!
WHY IS SHE IN THE BATHROOM AGAIN?
Conserve Water
HERE, FUKA.
ENGLISH/JAPANESE DICTIONARY
AKITO ASKED ME TO GIVE YOU THIS.
I SAW HIM IN THE HALL...
AH... THANKS, SANA...
SO, FUKA?
YEAH?
DID YOU KISS AKITO YET?
WHY D'YOU WANNA KNOW?
C'MON... YOU CAN TELL ME!
UH... NOT YET...
HUH ?
THAT SNEAKY PERV?
THE ONE WHO TOLD ME YOU SHOULD PAY ATTEN-TION TO THE ONE YOU LOVE? HIM?
NO. EVEN THOUGH WE'RE GOIN' OUT NOW...
...AND WHEN WE WERE FIVE, HE KISSED ME WHEN I DIDN'T WANT HIM TO...
HEE-HEE! BUT, YOU WANT HIM TO NOW?
UH...

WITH AKITO, ALL YOU NEED TO DO IS PUT YOUR FACE REALLY CLOSE TO HIS.
I'M SURE IF YOU DID, HE'D KISS YOU! OR TRY LEANING OVER HIM, I BET HE'D TRY TO FEEL YOU UP...
SHE'S JUST TEASING.
AND HOW DO YOU KNOW?
WELL, YOU KNOW...
OH NO! COUNTER-ATTACK!
WHAT??
ALL MEN ARE ALIKE. THEY'RE SO SIMPLE.
NICELY COUNTERED!
GIRL, YOU GOT NO RIGHT TO BE TALKIN' ABOUT MEN LIKE THAT.
AND WHY NOT?!
YOU CAN'T SAY "ALL MEN," UNLESS YOU'VE ACTUALLY GONE OUT WITH ALL OF 'EM.
AND YOU HAVEN'T GONE OUT WITH ANY.
LOOK, SANA AND FUKA ARE FIGHTING!
SO LET'S JUST END THIS CON-VERSATION RIGHT NOW.
ALL DONE!
OOH!! YOU'VE GOT SOME NERVE.
HMMM ...
PUT MY FACE CLOSE TO HIS...?
I'LL TRY IT!!
WHAAAT?

I SHOULDN'T HAVE OPENED MY MOUTH...
OKAY! 5 O'CLOCK, THEN!
RESULTS OF SELF-INFLICTED SABOTAGE
WHO KNEW THAT JUST JOKING AROUND, I'D END UP SABOTAGING MYSELF?
AT LEAST I LEARNED SOMETHING TODAY...
キーンコーン...
HEY, GIRL! TIME FOR GYMNASTICS!
ALL RIGHT! I'M READY!!
WHAT GOT YOU SO WORKED UP?
Auditorium 3
Gymnastics
CAPTAIN! I BROUGHT SANA KURATA WITH ME TODAY!
HELLO!
HELLO!
I'M SHIMIZU, THE CAPTAIN! I'M IN 8TH GRADE.
HEY, IT'S OUR PHANTOM MEMBER! HA HA!
AH... SORRY!

MM...
WOW!
THAT'S NICE!
ぶーん
AH! AH!
OOH, I CAN'T LOOK!
...
SHE DID IT!
GREAT!
くるんっ
すたっ
GO, FUKA!
SHE DID IT!
I'M TRYIN' TO CONCENTRATE, IDIOT! BE QUIET!
YOU SOUND LIKE A PERVERT AT A PEEP SHOW!
BUT FUKA, YOU'RE GREAT!
THAT WAS NOTHIN'!
FIRST, DO A HANDSTAND...
OKAY...
HEY, GREAT!
HUH?
BESIDES, CAN'T YOU DO ALL THAT STUFF? YOU MUSTA LEARNED IT AT KOMAWARI...
YOU GO THERE A LOT, RIGHT?
WELL...
I'M REALLY BETTER AT TUMBLING AND JUMPING... I DON'T THINK I COULD DO A PERFECT WALKOVER LIKE THAT.
REALLY?
SHE REALLY SHOWED UP!
SANA!

カラ
WHAT ARE YOU DOIN' HERE?
WE HEARD SANA WAS GOING TO COME TODAY! WE WANTED TO CHECK IT OUT.
さか さか さか さか さか さか
さか
ドキ ドキ
ズキ ズキ
フウ…
HE SNUCK UP ON ME AGAIN...
SANA! THAT WAS SO AMAZING!
ブチョー
SANA, FUKA DID REALLY WELL IN THE DISTRICT GYMNASTIC COMPETITION.
SHE WON THIRD PLACE!
BUT THEY COMPETE AS A TEAM, AND THE TEAM SCORE WASN'T VERY GOOD... SO SHE DIDN'T GET TO GO TO THE CITY MEET...
WHAT A SHAME.
NO BIGGIE! WE'LL DO IT NEXT YEAR!
BUT YOU'RE AMAZING, FUKA!
YOU COULD GET A GOLD MEDAL.
WELL, BEFORE I WAS BORN, MY MOM WAS A GYMNAST. SHE EVEN WENT TO THE OLYMPICS ...
THE OLYMPICS?!
GAZES OF ADMIRATION
SHE WASN'T A GREAT GYMNAST, BUT SHE LOVED BEING IN FRONT OF AN AUDIENCE...
ずる
SPIN, FUKA! SPIN!
ポーイ
HELP!!!
SO EVER SINCE I WAS REALLY LITTLE, SHE'S BEEN TRAINING ME AND TAKING ME TO DIFFERENT GYMNASTIC SCHOOLS...
WOW...
SO THAT'S HOW YOU GOT SO GOOD!
AND NOW THAT WE HAVE A REAL KOMAWARI GYMNAST LIKE YOU, SANA, WE'LL BE EVEN BETTER!
YOU TWO ARE GOING TO HELP MAKE THIS TEAM GREAT!

GO TEAM!
LET'S GO TO THE CITY MEET NEXT YEAR!
NOT SO EXCITED ABOUT THE IDEA...
YEAH!
WHA-?
I'M STARVED.
WANNA GET SOME-THING TO EAT?
IN OUR UNI-FORMS?
SURE! WHAT'S THE BIG DEAL?
SANA, DO YOU KNOW ABOUT FUKA AND AKITO? THEY'RE DATING NOW.
I HEARD...
SO, WHAT DO YOU THINK?
I WAS PRETTY SURPRISED TO HEAR IT...
...BUT, I GUESS IT'S OKAY...
HUH... "I GUESS IT'S OKAY?"
IT'S STICKING UP.
HUH?
AYA! LET ME FIX YOUR BOW!
PLEASE FIX IT!
AS TSUYOSHI SEES IT
I THINK THAT...
...AKITO HAS SEEMED REALLY LONELY...
...EVER SINCE HE STARTED GOING OUT WITH FUKA...

TWO MONTHS AGO
FUKA?
ARE YOU SERIOUS?
HOW DID THAT HAPPEN?
I DON'T GET IT...
WELL...
SHE ASKED ME TO GO OUT WITH HER...
WOULD YOU... BE MY BOYFRIEND?
WHEN WE WERE LITTLE, I DIDN'T LIKE YOU...
...BUT YOU'VE GROWN ON ME, I GUESS...
......
YOU DON'T GOTTA SAY YES...
...I JUST WANTED TO ASK...
....
I GUESS IT'S OKAY.
....
IT IS?
SURE.
....
UM... OKAY. GOTTA GO TO THE GYM.
LATER.
スタ スタ スタ

"I GUESS IT'S OKAY"?
YEAH.
THAT'S HOW I FELT ABOUT IT.
I'M TIRED.
AKITO? BUT WHAT ABOUT SANA?
GOTTA TAKE A NAP...
SANA...? SHE'S A BLOCKHEAD.
......
AND SHE HAS NAOZUMI. SHE'LL BE FINE.
IT'S TRUE.
AND I FIGURE ...
...I DON'T HATE FUKA...
WHEN HE TOLD ME...
...I WAS TAKEN ABACK.
IT MADE ME FEEL SAD...
EVER SINCE WE WERE IN 6TH GRADE, I FELT LIKE...
...THERE WAS SOMETHING REAL BETWEEN AKITO AND SANA.
A GENUINE BOND...

⑧
More from Me

Lately, a lot of readers have been getting mad at Sana, Akito, or Fuka over what's been happening in Kodocha... To Sana, they say: "Took you long enough to figure out you loved him!" To Akito: "What a fickle boy!" To Fuka: "How dare you try and steal Akito away from Sana." (This is the most common response.) But almost everyone has good things to say about Naozumi.

But the funny thing is, what most people have to say is, "I feel so bad for Sana, Akito and Fuka! Please hurry and work things out for them!"

You guys are all so nice! I thought you were going to blame me for all their problems!

I'm such a bad person. (Hee-hee!)

When I try to think about who the real villain in this triangle is... well, I don't think it's any of them. If you want to blame someone for the predicament they're in, you're gonna have to blame me!

ぷつ
ぷつ
ぷつ
だらーーん
......
WHAT'D YOU DO THAT FOR?
HE DID THE EXACT OPPOSITE ...
THAT LOOKS SO BAD! ARE YOU GONNA LEAVE IT LIKE THAT THE WHOLE DAY?
WHO DO YOU THINK YOU ARE, SHOWIN' OFF YOUR CHEST LIKE THAT? SOME TEEN IDOL OR BOY-BAND SINGER OR SOMETHIN'?
YOU LOOK STUPID!
クスクス
......
ちッ
ぷつ
きちん
WHY DIDN'T YOU JUST DO THAT IN THE FIRST PLACE?
WHAT D'YA THINK, GIRLS ARE GOING TO CHASE AFTER YOU OR SOMETHIN'?
SNORT!
あははは
クス...
あははは
IS THAT HOW THEY ALWAYS ACT?
PRETTY MUCH, YEAH.
AND FUKA WINS!!
IT'S KINDA FUNNY.
SO...
...I GUESS FUKA AND AKITO MAKE A GOOD COUPLE...
...AND SANA HAS NAOZUMI.
SO IT WORKED OUT FOR THE BEST FOR EVERYONE...
END OF TSUYOSHI'S VIEW ...

I FEEL LIKE SUCH A FIFTH WHEEL SITTING HERE!
HUH?
WELL, YOU GUYS ARE BOTH COUPLES!
AND I'M ALL BY MYSELF...
WELL, YOU CAN'T HELP THAT YOUR BOYFRIEND GOES TO ANOTHER SCHOOL!
YEAH! AND WE WANT YOU HERE WITH US, SILLY!
WE ALL MISSED YOU, AND WE'RE DYING TO HEAR EVERYTHING THAT HAPPENED.
YOU WERE ON A FILM SET! YOU MUST HAVE LOTS OF STORIES, AND YOU HAVEN'T TOLD US A THING!
HOLD IT!
WHAT BOYFRIEND?
OH, DON'T TRY TO FOOL US!
WE READ ALL ABOUT YOU AND NAOZUMI KAMURA! WE KNOW ALL ABOUT IT!
YEAH! YEAH!

WAIT... YOU ALL BELIEVED THAT STORY?
IT'S NOT TRUE!!
IT'S NOT?
NO WAY!
YOU MEAN...
...THOSE MAGAZINES MADE ALL THAT UP?
恋人宣言
THEY WERE ALL LIES!
AND, SINCE REI AND MR. MAEDA WERE IN THE MOUNTAINS WITH US, THEY COULDN'T DO ANY-THING UNTIL IT WAS TOO LATE.
THOSE REPORTERS JUST MADE THE WHOLE THING UP TO SELL COPIES!
IF WE'D ALL BEEN IN TOKYO, WE'D HAVE STOPPED IT FROM BEING PRINTED!!
AND YOU...
...YOU ALL BELIEVED THAT IT WAS TRUE?

BUT... ISHIDA...
HE SAID HE HEARD YOU TOLD HIM YOU WERE SEEING NAOZUMI...
ISHIDA?
ボーン
THAT MORON!
I TOLD HIM TO KEEP HIS MOUTH SHUT!
I ONLY TOLD HIM THAT SO I COULD TURN HIM DOWN WITHOUT HURTING HIS FEELINGS!
THAT'S ALL!
......
SO ALL OF YOU...
...YOU DIDN'T THINK TO ASK ME?
YOU JUST...
...BELIEVED THOSE STUPID MAGAZINES AND ISHIDA?

BUT, SANA! WHAT ELSE COULD WE THINK? YOU TWO GET ALONG SO WELL!
AND EVERYONE SAID IT WAS TRUE!
OF COURSE WE GET ALONG. WE'RE FRIENDS!
AND WE COULDN'T GET AHOLD OF YOU...
OF COURSE NOT! I WAS IN THE MOUNTAINS!
......
SANA...
I FEEL...
LIKE EVERYTHING GOOD...
BETWEEN...
I'LL DO MY BEST!
ME AND NAOZUMI...
I UNDER-STAND...
IT'S ALL BEEN TAINTED BY THIS...

NO...
NO...
OH, NO! I THINK I'M GOING TO CRY...
SANA?
....
SORRY, GUYS.
I REALLY HAVE TO GET GOING!
BUT, SANA!!
SANA!!

SANA!
COME BACK!
SANA!
バタバタ
ガタン
AKI...

!!
ぼろ
ぼろ
WHY ARE YOU CRYING?
WHAT DO YOU WANT?!
RELAX!
LET GO OF ME!
ぶん
ぶん

IS IT REALLY SO TRAGIC?
GO AWAY, OKAY?
NO!
LET ME GO!
SANA!
......
...?
AKITO ...

I TOLD YOU TO LET GO OF ME!!
DIDN'T I?
......
ダッ
DAMMIT!
I CAN'T BELIEVE THIS!

I HIT AKITO!
SHAKE
じん
じん
SHAKE
WELL, HE ASKED FOR IT.
BELIEVING THAT CRAP...
NOBODY KNOWS HOW I FEEL.
WELL...
...OF COURSE, IT'S NOT LIKE I'VE TALKED TO ANYONE.
I HAVEN'T TOLD THEM ANY-THING...
...SO HOW COULD THEY KNOW?

WELL, LOOKS LIKE NONE OF US CAN KEEP UP WITH SANA...
SHE SURE CAN RUN!
あはっ
YEAH, THE ONLY ONE FAST ENOUGH WAS AKITO.
HE'LL JUST HAVE TO REPRE-SENT US ALL.
THANKS, GUYS...
ふっ
...FOR TRYING.
IT'S NOTHING!
AHA! HE'S BACK!
WHERE'S SANA?
SHE YELLED AT ME, SLAPPED ME, AND THEN RAN HOME.
ヒリ ヒリ ヒリ
...しーーん...
WHAT'S WITH HER?
I DON'T GET HER AT ALL ...
WOW, ANOTHER NICE HANDPRINT FOR HIS COLLECTION...
OOH, THAT'S GOTTA HURT...
......
HA
I'M SUCH AN IDIOT.

I KNEW HOW BAD RUMORS COULD HURT PEOPLE...
...AFTER WHAT HAPPENED TO ME.
BUT THE RUMORS ABOUT SANA WERE SO BELIEVABLE...
HOW STUPID!
....
LATER, GUYS!
SO SANA'S NOT GOIN' OUT...
...WITH THAT GUY AFTER ALL.
WHAT ARE YOU GONNA DO?
WHAT I'M ALREADY DOIN'.
I'M GOIN' OUT WITH YOU, SO IT'S NOT MY PROBLEM, IS IT?

......
YEAH, REMEMBER WHEN YOU BORROWED THAT CD LAST MONTH? I ASKED YOU TO GIVE IT BACK THE NEXT DAY AND YOU STILL HAVE IT!
YEAH ... AND ...
AND YOU SAY WE'RE GOIN' OUT, BUT ALL WE DO IS WALK HOME FROM SCHOOL TOGETHER!
EXCEPT WHEN YOU HAVE KARATE!
I WANNA BELIEVE YOU...
...BUT I'M NOT GONNA.
YOU'RE NOT GONNA?
GETTING HER ACCENT →
WE HAVE BEEN ON TWO DATES, BUT THEY WERE BOTH DOUBLE DATES WITH AYA AND TSUYOSHI.
ぶつ
ぶつ
ぶつ
STAY RIGHT THERE!!
だっ
しゅ
HUH? WHA-?
......
WHERE...?
WELL, THERE HE GOES AGAIN ...
ひゅう...

9

Big Changes

To Sana, it seemed like Akito got gigantic overnight! (Hee-hee!) But sometimes people really can grow up to four inches a year when they're at that age. And people change in other ways, too—sometimes people's whole attitude can change during just a single month away on vacation. And when you see them again, it's like, "What happened to you?"

When I came back for the second semester of high school, that's what everyone said to me!

I think the main reason Akito grew so fast that year is because he slept a lot. Also, up until the sixth grade, he really didn't eat well at all. So when things got better at home and he started to eat properly, his body suddenly got all the nutrition it had been needing!

Eating well is very important—especially during a growth spurt. Sometimes, girls start dieting while they're still growing. But please don't do that to yourself! You shouldn't worry about diets at that age anyway, because just being young makes you automatically cute! (Hee-hee!)

And besides, it's what's inside that counts!

Although I have to confess that for eight years now, I've been planning to go on a diet... but I still haven't done it!

AND THEN WHEN ALL THOSE STORIES CAME OUT ABOUT SANA...
倉田紗南
恋人宣言
...HE SEEMED SO SAD AND LONELY, AND I FELT SO BAD FOR HIM.
WOULD YOU BE MY BOY-FRIEND FOR REAL?
THIS IS HOW FUKA SAW HIM
I ORIGINALLY ASKED HIM TO GO OUT WITH ME...
...BECAUSE I FELT BAD FOR HIM...
!?
HUH? MY CD?
YOU RAN ALL THE WAY HOME TO GET THIS FOR ME?
THAT WAS FAST.
YUP, AND I BEAT TWO GUYS UP ON THE WAY BACK.
WHAT?!
I'M JOKING...
THE TRUTH IS...
...THAT I'VE FALLEN IN LOVE WITH HIM.

This is my last space in this volume. Thanks for reading everything!

As I told you in this volume, from book 7 on, things are going to get a lot more serious in Kodocha. I'm a little nervous about it because I know a lot of you have said you don't want things to get too dark! But I think that I have to write it my own way and see what happens.

I've done some serious storylines in Kodocha before, but not quite like this—when things as serious as a person's "true love" come along, it's very easy to sympathize with what's happening...and I'm sure the readers will be anxious and worried along with the characters. I feel that way, too! When Sana is feeling blue, I start getting depressed myself!

But, well, it wouldn't be a good story if it didn't have some serious parts, right? So it'll be okay.

Please keep following the story of Sana and her friends for just a little while longer!

And...

SANA CAME HOME CRYING?
YEAH... HER FACE WAS ALL BLOTCHY.
SHE MUST HAVE BEEN REALLY UPSET.
OH... TO BE YOUNG!
IT'S ALRIGHT... LET HER SOB AWAY!
IT WILL HELP HER GROW UP A LITTLE MORE.
WHAT KIND OF REACTION IS THAT?
SHE'S SO STRANGE...
I'M SO MIXED UP.
MY OWN FRIENDS BELIEVED THOSE TABLOIDS...
...JUST LIKE THOSE GIRLS WHO BEAT ME UP.
I FELT SO STRANGE SITTING THERE IN THE CAFÉ WITH THEM TODAY.
HOW CAN IT BE SO PAINFUL...
...TO BE AT SCHOOL, OR WITH MY "FRIENDS"...?
コンコン
SANA?

SANA, THERE'S A BIG MEETING FOR CHILD'S TOY TODAY. THEY'D LIKE YOU TO COME.
HUH? WHAT FOR?
I'M NOT SURE. I THINK THEY WANT TO DO AN HOUR-LONG SPECIAL.
RIGHT... I HEARD ABOUT THAT...
IF YOU CAN'T GO, I'LL GO INSTEAD...
NO, NO!
I'LL GO! IT'S MY JOB, AFTER ALL.
JUST LET ME CHANGE...
I HAVEN'T APPEARED ON CHILD'S TOY IN AGES BECAUSE OF THE MOVIE.
I BET MR. YONMA MISSES ME!
HE PLAYS HER TEACHER
HELLO!
OH, HI!!
IT'S MR. MAEDA!
HELLO!

IS NAOZUMI HERE WITH YOU?
YEAH, IN THE DRESSING ROOM.
え
I'LL BE RIGHT BACK!
HEY, SANA! JEEZ...
NAOZUMI! YOU'RE NOT GONNA BELIEVE THIS!
わーっ
SANA! I'M IN THE MIDDLE OF CHANGING...
I HAVE TO TELL YOU...
NAOZUMI!
バーン
!?
WHAT TH-
!?
OH, IT'S YOU.
がばっ
ULP
ARE THOSE... SCARS FROM YOUR BURNS?
UH... YEAH...
I HAD FOR-GOT-TEN... WHEN I CAME OUT OF THE HOUSE...
OKAY!
SANA! ARE YOU OKAY?
...HE PROTECTED ME FROM THE FIRE.
NAOZUMI...

...WAS SO SWEET TO ME...
...BACK THERE.
スポーン
MAYBE WE SHOULD HAVE...
...REALLY GONE OUT, LIKE THE REPORTERS SAID.
UM... SANA...
HUH?
IF SOMEONE SEES US LIKE THIS...
...THE RUMORS ARE GOING TO START AGAIN.
IT'S NICE, THOUGH.
OH, I DON'T CARE WHAT THEY SAY ANYMORE.
PRESS
LET'S ABANDON THIS WORLD TO SEARCH FOR OUR VERY OWN SHANGRI-LA!
LET'S GO!
WHAT ARE YOU DOING?
SANA! SNAP OUT OF IT!
WHAT'S WRONG? DID SOMETHING HAPPEN?
YEAH.
I CAN'T BELIEVE I CHANGED IN FRONT OF YOU.
WHAT WAS IT?

WELL, I DON'T KNOW IF I CAN TALK TO YOU ABOUT IT.
IT MIGHT BE INSENSITIVE.
I SEE!
SO EVERYONE BELIEVED THOSE ARTICLES...
YEAH, EVEN MY FRIENDS.
I WAS SO UPSET!
OH, PUH-LEAZE ...
YOU'VE NEVER BEEN WORRIED ABOUT BEING INSENSITIVE BEFORE!
YOU CAN TALK TO ME.
I GUESS YOU'RE RIGHT.
AND, HEY, KNOWING YOU'RE INSENSITIVE IS PROGRESS!
......
......
THIS DOESN'T ADD UP.
HUH?
DID AKITO START GOING OUT WITH THAT GIRL BEFORE...
...OR AFTER THE ARTICLES CAME OUT?
HUH?
I DUNNO.
WHAT'S THE DIFFERENCE?
......
SHE'S AS DENSE AS EVER.
KAMURA! TIME TO GET GOING!

I'M SORRY, SANA. GOTTA GO.
OH, NO, I'M SORRY FOR BUSTING IN HERE.
OH! WHAT ARE YOU TAPING TODAY?
I'M GOING ON A TALK SHOW TO PROMOTE "MANSION OF WATER."
MY SEGMENT WILL RUN TOMORROW-TRY AND WATCH, OKAY?
SURE! GOOD LUCK!
REI! SORRY ABOUT THAT!
C'MON, THEY'RE STARTING.
WE'RE PLANNING A SPECIAL EPISODE OF "CHILD'S TOY," AND WE WANT TO DO...
...A SPECIAL SEGMENT FOR SANA BEING BACK...
I'M HERE!
YOU DON'T HAVE TO SAY IT NOW...
...BUT THANKS FOR REMIND-ING US.
WE WANT TO TAPE YOUR SEGMENT TOMOR-ROW.
TOMOR-ROW?
SO SOON?
ALL RIGHT...

1 - 8
キーンコーン
SANA ONLY CAME TO SCHOOL FOR ONE DAY.
I GUESS SHE'S OUT FOR WORK AGAIN.
I WONDER IF SHE'LL QUIT SCHOOL ENTIRELY.
SANA'S DESK.
BUT I'LL TAKE SOME NOTES FOR HER ANYWAY.
THAT'LL MAKE HER HAPPY.
WELCOME BACK SANA!
STAR OF THE MOVIE "MANSION OF THE WATER!" ALREADY A MOVIE QUEEN?
MR. YONMA!
A LOT OF YOUNG ACTORS HAVE JOINED THE CAST WHILE I WAS GONE!
RECORDING "KODOCHA"
THAT'S BECAUSE MOST OF THE KIDS GRADUATED, BUT YOU GOT HELD BACK!
WHAT DOES "LEFT BACK" MEAN?
アハハ
DID YOU JUST MAKE FUN OF ME?
THIS IS BAD.
CUT! CUT!
BUT YOU'RE REALLY SHOWING OFF TODAY. DO YOU THINK YOU'RE SACHIKO KOBAYASHI?*
OK, LET'S TRY A GAME NOW.
ぼよ〜〜ん
あははは
MR. YONMA, YOU CALL THIS A MATCH?
キャハハハ
HERE! HERE!
JUST KEEP GOING, SANA!
GO FOR IT!

*SACHIKO KOBAYASHI IS A VERY POPULAR SINGER, FAMOUS FOR HER FLASHY STYLE AND COSTUMES.

キャー
GOT IT! GOT IT!
あ〜
THE GOAL IS THAT WAY!
だーっ
SANA!
ドタタ
A HA HA HA HA!
I HAD SO MUCH FUN TODAY! ♬
YOU LOOKED LIKE YOU WERE HAVING A GOOD TIME.
ブオー
IT'S GREAT TO HAVE A FUN JOB!
YOU THINK SO?
I'M GLAD.
I'M STARTING TO THINK THAT MAYBE I SHOULD JUST FOCUS ON MY WORK.
SCHOOL IS TOO HARD RIGHT NOW...
MANAGING IS FUN, TOO!
ブオー
I'M NOT TELLING REI YET.
HE'D SIGN ME UP FOR TOO MUCH WORK AND KILL ME!
I'M HOME!
HELLO, SANA.
NAOZUMI IS ON TV.
HE'S TALKING ABOUT YOUR MOVIE.

OH, YEAH! THE TALK SHOW HE WAS DOING YESTERDAY! ♪ I GOTTA SEE THIS.
THE LOCATION MUST HAVE BEEN HARD.
IT SURE WAS!
NOW I HAVE A NEW APPRECIATION OF THINGS LIKE ELECTRICITY!
HA HA.
THERE'VE BEEN A LOT OF RUMORS ABOUT YOU AND SANA KURATA.
MAY I ASK YOU ABOUT THEM ...?
YEAH, SURE!
ドキ
UH-OH!!
THEY'RE TALKING ABOUT ME?
LOOKS LIKE IT!
ホホッ
MARO
WELL, ABOUT THESE ARTICLES ...
...THOSE ARE ALL LIES!
AND THEY CAUSED US SO MUCH TROUBLE BECAUSE PEOPLE BELIEVED THEM!
I ADMIT, I LIKED SANA...
...BUT THE TRUTH IS, SHE TURNED ME DOWN.
NO WAY!
GASP!
DO YOU REALLY WANT TO TALK ABOUT IT, NAOZUMI?
YEAH, SURE.
WE COULD CUT ...
SURE ?...?
NO, NAOZUMI! DON'T TALK ABOUT IT!
HE'S TOO HONEST!
MAYBE YOU SHOULDN'T BE SO HONEST ...
NAOZUMI!! WHAT ABOUT YOUR DECENCY ?
I THINK YOU MEAN "DIGNITY," SANA!
ホホホ
MARO

IT TURNED OUT SHE ALREADY REALLY LIKED SOMEONE.
WHAT?
GASP!
NAOZUMI!!
HOW DARE YOU!
WOW! THIS IS A SCOOP!! IS HE AN ACTOR, TOO?
NO, HE'S NOT. AND I CAN'T TELL YOU WHO HE IS...
HOW CAN YOU DO THIS?!
REALLY ...?
SANA, THERE'S NO POINT IN YELLING.
THIS WAS TAPED YESTERDAY, REMEMBER?
BUT I'LL GIVE YOU A HINT.
THE MORNING WE LEFT FOR LOCATION, HE CAME BY TO SEE HER OFF.

HUH? WELL, THAT DOESN'T TELL ME ANY-THING...
THAT'S OKAY, YOU DON'T NEED TO KNOW WHO IT IS.
BUT THAT'S WHAT SANA TOLD ME, SO I KNOW IT'S TRUE.
WELL, THAT SOUNDS SERI-OUS...
SO EVEN THOUGH YOU WORK TOGETHER ALL THE TIME...
...THERE'S NOTHING GOING ON?
THAT'S THE TRUTH...
CUT!
CUT NOW!
CUT! CUT!
IT'S DONE!
TOO LATE!!
AND IT WAS SEEN ALL OVER THE COUN-TRY...
AAAAAGH!!

HE'LL KNOW!
EVEN IF NO ONE ELSE CAN FIGURE IT OUT, HE WILL!
I'LL DO MY BEST, TOO.
AKITO...
NOW HE KNOWS...
THAT I LIKE...
HIM...
REI?
WHERE'S NAOZUMI RIGHT NOW?
PROBABLY AT HOME... MR. MAEDA SAID HE HAD TODAY OFF.
GET THE CAR!
YEP!
OH, HELLO!
THIS IS A SURPRISE!

LOOK, MR. MAEDA! NOW I HAVE GIRLS VISITING IN THE MIDDLE OF THE NIGHT!
HA HA HA HA
YOU'RE REALLY GROWING UP!
HA HA HA HA
......
がしっ
THIS ISN'T FUNNY, NAOZUMI...
STOP IT!
SO VIOLENT!
WHAT DID YOU SAY
OOH, SHE'S MAD... ♡
DO YOU LIKE OTHER PEOPLE TO TALK ABOUT HOW YOU FEEL?
ESPECIALLY ON TV?
NO.
IT'S JUST JUICE
......!!
THEN WHY DID YOU DO IT TO ME?
......
SANA...
DIDN'T YOU THINK...

...THAT I MIGHT BE...
...JUST A LITTLE HURT...
...WHEN YOU TURNED ME DOWN?
......
SO I THINK YOU CAN FORGIVE ME FOR A LITTLE TEASING...
......
ぷっ
THAT'S NOT THE POINT!
......
HE HAS A GIRLFRIEND!
I DON'T WANT HIM TO KNOW HOW I FEEL!
DIDN'T I TELL YOU THAT ON THE MOUNTAIN?
AND HIS GIRLFRIEND IS MY FRIEND!
YOU DIDN'T THINK ABOUT HER FEELINGS AT ALL, DID YOU?
BUT I DON'T KNOW HER.
しれっ

BESIDES, YOU'RE THE ONE THAT DOESN'T THINK ABOUT OTHER PEOPLE'S FEELINGS...
YOU DON'T EVEN REALIZE THAT AKITO LIKES YOU.
WHAT?
I'M SURE HE'S FELT THAT WAY SINCE BEFORE YOU WENT ON LOCATION.
NO! THAT'S NOT TRUE!
HOW DO YOU KNOW?
AND HOW DO YOU?
SANA, EVERY-BODY KNOWS IT EXCEPT YOU!
......
I DON'T BELIEVE IT!
I WON'T BELIEVE IT UNTIL HE TELLS ME HIMSELF!
THEN WHY DON'T YOU ASK HIM?
......
SO THAT'S THE KIND OF PERSON YOU ARE...
EVIL BRAT!

ぶっちんっ
...NEVER SPEAKING TO YOU AGAIN!
NAOZUMI ...
...I'M...
ぷる
ぷる
ぷる
......
ふっ
バタタタタ
バタン
SHE'S NOT SPEAKING TO ME...
HOW SAD...
だ
I HOPE SOMEDAY SHE UNDERSTANDS.
パプ
I ONLY DID IT BECAUSE ...
すっ
...I'M ON HER SIDE.
YEAH! PLAY IT, NAOZUMI!
STOP THAT RACKET!!!
STUPID NAO-ZUMI!
WOW, THAT MUST HAVE BEEN SOME FIGHT... WISH I'D SEEN IT...
HE WAS IN THE CAR
ブオー

I REALLY CAN'T HANDLE SCHOOL RIGHT NOW.
CAN'T WE GO SOMEWHERE FOR THE DAY?
THE BEACH, MAYBE?
WHEN YOU'RE NOT AT WORK, YOU GO TO SCHOOL!
I NEED A BREAK!!
DON'T BE A BABY!
THAT MORNING, SHE LOST TO HER MOTHER.
REI...
BUT YOU KNOW WHAT YOUR MOTHER SAID: IF YOU'RE NOT WORKING, YOU HAVE TO GO...
HEY, CHEER UP. MAYBE NO ONE EVEN SAW THE INTERVIEW.
AT LEAST MAYBE AKITO DIDN'T...
NAOZUMI KNEW THAT WAS PRIVATE...
WELL, AKITO DIDN'T TELL ANYONE THAT HE SAW YOU OFF THAT DAY, RIGHT?
SO NO ONE ELSE WILL KNOW HE'S THE ONE NAOZUMI WAS TALKING ABOUT.
SO AS LONG AS YOU'RE NOT ALONE WITH HIM, EVERYTHING WILL BE FINE.
OKAY?
......
HUH?
HE'S RIGHT!
NO ONE ELSE KNOWS...
AS LONG AS I STAY AWAY FROM AKITO, I'LL BE FINE!
I'M SURE I CAN DO IT FOR AT LEAST ONE DAY!
LIKE A GAME.
1-8
1-7
MORNING, SANA!
WHAT'S UP?
MORNING!
MY CLASSROOM IS FAR AWAY FROM HIS...
...SO I CAN AVOID HIM IF I WANT TO!
YES!!
READY... —GAME START—.

MORNIN', SANA!
YOU'RE EARLY TODAY.
WHASSUP!
LIKE A TOUGH GUY
SO, WHAT DID YOU DO LAST NIGHT?
HUH? LAST NIGHT?
MY MOM RENTED US A VIDEO.
IT WAS SO CUTE!
ALL RIGHT! AT LEAST FUKA DIDN'T SEE IT.
LEVEL CLEAR!
キーンコーン
ピー!!
OKAY, EVERYBODY! LET'S GO!
A GROUP ATTACK
SANA!
NAOZUMI KAMURA TALKED ABOUT YOU LAST NIGHT!
DID YOU SEE IT?
DID YOU REALLY TURN HIM DOWN?
UH-OH...
DON'T SAY IT!
HUH? SANA...
THERE'S SOMEONE YOU LIKE?
NOT THAT NAOZUMI GUY?
....
WHY DIDN'T YOU TELL ME?
SO WHO IS IT THAT YOU REALLY LIKE?
UH... IT'S...

......
NO! I CAN'T TELL YOU.
AND BESIDES, YOU KNOW YOU CAN'T BELIEVE WHAT ACTORS SAY.
EVEN THOUGH I'M AN ACTRESS.
YUP!
くりっ
WHO IS IT? TELL US!
?
YOU SHOULDN'T BELIEVE GOSSIP, SHOULD YOU?
SHE'S RIGHT.
BUT IS IT...?
BUT I LIKE GOSSIP!
うふっ
C'MON! LET'S STOP TALKING...
...AND START PLAYING BALL!
バリボー バリボー!!
シュルルル
フゥ
LEVEL CLEAR!
YOU HEARD SANA...
HUH?
LET ME TAKE YOU TO THE NURSE'S OFFICE!
NO, I'M FINE!
KEEP PLAYING!
じゃっ
AT LAST, I CAN GET OUT OF HERE!
タタッ
HMPF!
バシッ
LET'S EXERCISE!
I'M SO SORRY!
ARE YOU OKAY?
UUUUUHH...
I THINK YOUR FINGER'S JAMMED...
WEREN'T YOU LOOKING?

CLINIC
OKAY, YOU SHOULD BE FINE NOW.
THANK YOU!
WHAT A BUMMER.
MY LIFE IS SO HARD ...
ARE YOU OKAY?
DO YOU FEEL SICK ?
WELL, I'VE GOT A CRAMP ...
A LIE
CAN I REST FOR A BIT?
A LIAR
OF COURSE ...
IF YOU'RE IN PAIN, REST IS BEST!
HEE-HEE!
I'LL JUST STAY HERE 'TIL SCHOOL'S OVER.
UH OH !!
LET ME GET YOU SOME-THING FOR THAT...
OKAY! ♡
SOMEONE'S IN THE NEXT BED, SO BE QUIET.
SURE ...
OOPS...I WOKE HIM UP.
むく...

シャッ
....
ドカーン
GAME OVER.
ポリ...
....
FROZEN
......
UM...
WH...
WHAT'S WRONG?
?
ボー...

I DIDN'T GET ANY SLEEP LAST NIGHT.
HE'S OUT OF IT.
NURSE, I'M FINE!
I'LL BE GOING.
I WAS SO TIRED ...
...I FELL RIGHT OUT OF MY CHAIR IN CLASS.
HOW AWFUL!
WHAT? BUT HERE'S YOUR MEDI-CINE...
THAT'S OKAY! THANKS FOR EVERY-THING!
OH... OH...
THAT WAS CLOSE!
!!

......
ガタン
...NAOZUMI...
LAST NIGHT ON TV...
...SAID SOMETHING STRANGE.
I COULDN'T BELIEVE MY EARS.

BUT I...
...COULDN'T STOP THINKING...
...ABOUT WHETHER IT WAS TRUE OR NOT.
....
SO TELL ME THE TRUTH...
I WON'T BELIEVE IT...
...UNTIL I HEAR IT FROM YOU.
THE...
...TRUTH?
KODOCHA: SANA'S STAGE 6/THE END

HMPH

Kodocha Extra Comic

An Egg Full of Thorns

Obana tells a story about the Hayama family.

AT BIRTH, A PERSON'S HEART...
...IS AS SMOOTH AS AN EGG.
つるん
SNACK TIME!
YAY!
EAT UP, NOW.
HAYAMA
ばちんっ
!
AKITO AT 3 ...
PUDDING ...
FOR AS LONG AS AKITO CAN REMEMBER ...
NATSUMI AT 6 ...
GO SIT OVER THERE!
...... OWIE...
...HIS SISTER HAD BEEN MEAN TO HIM.
BUT HE DIDN'T KNOW WHY.

......
!
AAGGH!
AAAAGGH!
THEIR FATHER'S HOUSEKEEPER TOOK CARE OF THEM EVERY DAY.
HER NAME WAS MISS NOGUCHI.
TSK... AKITO, WHAT ARE YOU DOING NOW?
I'VE GOT A LOT TO DO TODAY. DON'T GIVE ME ANY TROUBLE...
NATSUMI, DID YOU DO SOMETHING TO AKITO?
NO, NOTHING!
HE FELL ALL BY HIMSELF.
OF COURSE YOU DIDN'T DO ANYTHING, YOU'RE SUCH A GOOD GIRL!
YEAH! BUT AKITO'S A DUMMY.
COME AND HELP ME, OKAY?
OKAY!
AKITO DID KNOW...
...THAT AS LONG AS HE DIDN'T COMPLAIN ABOUT NATSUMI PICKING ON HIM, NOTHING REALLY BAD WOULD HAPPEN.

……
ぐり…
BUT BIT BY BIT...
BIT BY BIT...
SPITE
SORROW
ANGER
PAIN
THORNS BEGAN TO GROW ON HIS HEART.
DADDY! YOU'RE HOME!
HELLO, KIDS.
THEIR FATHER WORKED LATE ALMOST EVERY NIGHT, SO HE DIDN'T SPEND MUCH TIME WITH AKITO AND HIS SISTER.
WHERE'S MISS NOGUCHI?
SHE JUST LEFT.
AH.

NATSUMI ALWAYS MONOPOLIZED WHAT LITTLE TIME THEIR FATHER SPENT WITH THEM.
DID YOU HAVE A GOOD DAY?
YEAH!
WE HAD SNACKS!
AND I HAD A BATH!
I GOT IN BY MYSELF.
AKITO COULD ONLY GET HIS UNDIVIDED ATTENTION WHEN THEY TOOK THEIR NIGHTLY BATH.
AKITO!
BATH TIME!
CAN YOU COUNT TO TEN?
ONE—
TWO—
THREE
TEN
UH... NOT QUITE...
AKITO WANTED TO TALK TO HIS DAD ABOUT THE WAY NATSUMI ACTED...
MMMM... DADDY?
WHAT, AKITO?
AHH...
...NUFFINK.
ぶくぶく
WHAT IS IT?
SLEEPY?
EVERY NIGHT, WHEN HIS FATHER ASKED IF HE HAD A GOOD DAY, AKITO WANTED TO TELL HIM THE TRUTH.
BUT HE WAS AFRAID THAT THE TRUTH WOULD JUST DISAPPOINT HIS FATHER... AND SO HE NEVER SAID A WORD.
ONE DAY, WHEN MISS NOGUCHI WENT SHOPPING AND LEFT AKITO AND NATSUMI ALONE...
どんっ

......
WHY ...
むく...
ズキ
ズキ
...AKITO FINALLY FOUGHT BACK!!
WHY? WHY YOU... ...HIT ME ... ...AND PUSH ME...?
WHY?! MEANIE! PIG!
WHAT?
HOW DARE YOU TALK TO ME THAT WAY?
...IN A 3-YEAR-OLD'S FASHION ...
LITTLE BRAT!
I DO IT BECAUSE I HATE YOU!
BABY BOY
MOM LEFT TO HAVE YOU, AND SHE NEVER CAME BACK!
SHE DIED!
AND THAT DAY, HE FOUND OUT WHERE THEIR MOTHER HAD GONE...
AND IT'S YOUR FAULT! I HATE YOU!
AND DADDY HATES YOU, TOO!

HE DIDN'T REALLY UNDERSTAND WHAT HIS SISTER WAS SAYING, OR WHAT DYING REALLY MEANT... BUT HE DID UNDERSTAND THE LAST WORDS HIS SISTER SAID.
"AND DADDY HATES YOU, TOO!"
...AND THORN AFTER THORN...
...GREW ON HIS HEART...
SORROW
SPITE
WHY?
CONFUSION
PAIN
ANGER
FEAR
HATE
NO!
HELLO, DADDY!
HUH? WHERE'S AKITO?
I DUNNO.
WHO CARES...
HELLO, KIDS—
AKITO?
C'MON, BATHTIME...
ガチャ...

"AND DADDY HATES YOU, TOO!"
キライ
きらい
キライ
UMM, DADDY... I GONNA ...
...TAKE MY BATH BY MYSELF NOW.
ALL BY YOURSELF?
YOU'RE SURE?
UH-HUH ...
AND THAT DAY...
...AKITO CLOSED UP HIS HEART...
パタン…
"AND DADDY HATES YOU TOO!"
AKITO ...
TOO LATE
パタ
パタ
パタ
BECAUSE OF HIS DOUBTS AND FEARS, AKITO COULDN'T TALK TO HIS FATHER... AND BECAUSE OF HIS SILENCE, AKITO'S FATHER...
...CAME TO HAVE HIS OWN DOUBTS AND FEARS, AS WELL.
DOES AKITO... HATE ME?!
ガガー
BUT AS USUAL, AKITO'S FATHER WAS TIRED AND DISTRACTED... AND DECIDED IT WAS PROBABLY NOTHING. SO HE JUST LET AKITO GO.
HMM-MM...
ARE THERE "TERRIBLE THREES?"
IT DIDN'T SEEM LIKE MUCH, BUT IT WAS JUST THE BEGINNING...

AFTER A WHILE, THEY BARELY SPOKE TO EACH OTHER (AND AKITO BARELY SPOKE AT ALL)...
...AND THE DISTANCE BETWEEN THE THREE HAYAMAS GREW GREATER AND GREATER.
ALL THREE BORE THEIR SHARE OF THE BLAME.
AKITO SHUT HIMSELF OFF COMPLETELY BECAUSE HE BELIEVED THAT HIS SISTER AND FATHER HATED HIM.
AH
I MUST GO ON...
HIS FATHER KEPT HIMSELF TOO BUSY TO REALLY PAY ATTENTION TO HIS CHILDREN... BECAUSE HE COULDN'T FACE THE GRIEF HE FELT AFTER LOSING HIS WIFE.
AND EVEN NATSUMI, WHO WAS TRYING TO HURT AKITO... ONLY DID IT BECAUSE SHE SO DESPERATELY LOVED AND MISSED HER MOTHER.
わーん
まま
MOMMY!
THEY ALL WERE DRIVEN TO DO WHAT THEY DID BY LOVE...
...BUT THIS LOVE WAS BEING TWISTED, LITTLE BY LITTLE.
OH, DEAR ...
WHAT IS HAP-PENING TO YOU ALL?
しーーん...
AND THE SADDEST OF THEM ALL WAS AKITO'S MOTHER, WATCHING OVER THEM FROM ABOVE...
羽山
BY THE TIME HE WAS 5, AKITO HAD BECOME THE LITTLE BRAT AND LONER WHO SANA WOULD MEET...
HMPH!
HE'S ALWAYS TELLING LIES!
HE'S NEVER ON TIME!

HEY, SOMEONE AT WORK GAVE ME TICKETS TO THE BIG DINOSAUR EXHIBIT... WOULD YOU LIKE TO GO?
YEAH! YEAH!
TRIP WITH DADDY...
HM.
WILL AKITO WANT TO...
WHY ASK? LET'S GO!
BAH!
SO, THE HAYAMA FAMILY WENT TO THE BIG DINOSAUR SHOW.
IT WAS QUITE REMARKABLE FOR THEM TO DO ANYTHING TOGETHER, OTHER THAN VISIT THEIR MOTHER'S GRAVE...
Dinosaur Exhibit
See all the dinosaurs!!
Welcome
......
......
ざわ
ざわ
WOW

どや
どや
OOF!
OOF!
ムギュ
SO MANY...
AKITO?
WHERE ARE YOU?
AGH...
CAN'T GET...
...THROUGH...
わた
わた
I'VE GOT YOU.
順路
SHOP
DADDY! I WANT THAT!
WHAT?
......

AND... THAT ONE!!
AKITO, DON'T YOU WANT SOME-THING?
......
YOUR SISTER IS GETTING TWO...
...SO YOU PICK OUT TWO THAT YOU LIKE, OKAY?
こくん
THESE TWO.
ALL THESE, PLEASE.
......
HERE!
AKITO...

AKITO WAS...
...VERY HAPPY THAT DAY.
BUT HE NEVER TOLD HIS FATHER ...
...AND HIS FATHER NEVER KNEW.
C'MON, KIDS...
ON THE WAY HOME, HIS FATHER TRIED TO CHEER AKITO UP.
AKITO ...
HE THOUGHT JOKING AROUND WOULD MAKE HIM SMILE.
ガタタン
ガタタン
DO YOU KNOW WHAT THOSE ARE?
ガタタン
ガタタン
...?
THOSE ARE DINOSAUR EGGS.
!

プギャー
DON'T BE SILLY, DADDY!
NO FOOLING HER...
ガタタン
......
WOULD AKITO BELIEVE IT...?
NAH...
ガタタン
...BUT AKITO BELIEVED HIM.
AND WHEN HE TOLD HIS FRIENDS, THEY LAUGHED...
TSUYOSHI! TSUYOSHI!
I SAW THE DINOSAUR EGGS!
THESE?
HA HA HA!
THOSE ARE JUST GIANT GAS TANKS!
がーん
DADDY... LIED TO ME?
THE THORNS GREW
...AND AKITO'S PAIN AND CONFUSION GREW DEEPER AND DEEPER...

THE STORY OF HOW AKITO OPENED UP TO HIS FATHER...
...IS A STORY THAT BEGAN WHEN AKITO MET A CERTAIN GIRL...
"CERTAIN GIRL"
...AND IT SHOWS HOW SUCH A HUGE MISUNDERSTANDING...
...CAN BE RESOLVED WITH JUST A LITTLE LOVE AND HOPE.
A HEART...
...MAY GROW MANY THORNS...
CROWDING

...IT MAY GROW MORE AND MORE THORNS THROUGHOUT LIFE...
BUT, AS MORE THORNS GROW...
...ONE DAY THERE WILL BE SO MANY, THE HEART WILL BECOME SMOOTH AND ROUND AGAIN...
TRULY, THAT'S WHAT WILL HAPPEN.
EVERYTHING WILL BE OKAY.
AHAHA
AND NOW, BACK TO THE PRESENT...
HEY, DAD!
WHEN I WAS A KID, YOU LIED TO ME! YOU OLD BRAGGART!
C'MON! TELL THE TRUTH!
LIED ABOUT WHAT?
DON'T WORRY ABOUT WHAT HAPPENED YEARS AGO...
CALM DOWN...
LIAR! YOU TOLD ME THE GAS TANKS WERE...
HAYAMA
AND TODAY, AKITO HAS THREE TOY DINOSAURS HE LOVES.

Coming Next!

What is Kodocha? It's the smash-hit comedy series from Japan about what happens when child star Sana Kurata tries to "fix" the problems of everyone around her. And there are a LOT of problems to solve. Sana and Hayama have finally admitted that they like each other...but, unfortunately, Fuka heard their confession. Since Sana doesn't want to betray her friend, she decides to tell Hayama she doesn't like him anymore. They try to move on—but Sana and Hayama just can't forget each other. Hayama's grades drop and his relationship with Fuka hits the skids. Just when things look like they can't get any worse, a guy named Kamori threatens suicide when Hayama refuses to be his friend. Hayama goes to find him, and Sana prays everything works out before someone loses their mind...or their life.

TOKYOPOP
Meet Misaki, the Prodigy.
A lightning-fast fighting doll.
An insane mentor.
A pinky promise to be the best.
ANGELIC LAYER
The new manga from CLAMP, creators of Cardcaptor Sakura.
Available now!
100% AUTHENTIC MANGA
品質第一公式商品

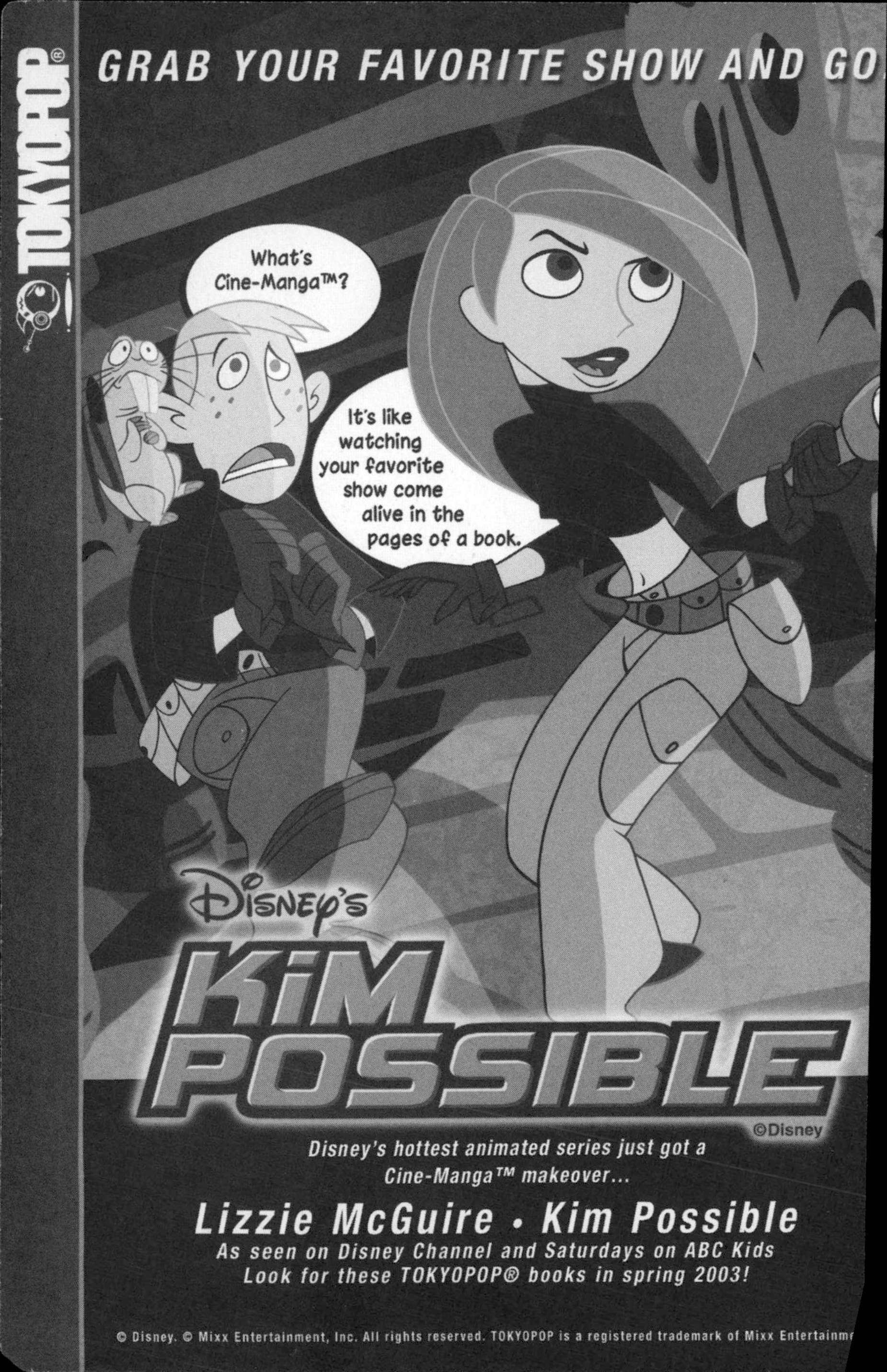
TOKYOPOP®
GRAB YOUR FAVORITE SHOW AND GO
What's Cine-Manga™?
It's like watching your favorite show come alive in the pages of a book.
Disney's
Kim Possible
©Disney
Disney's hottest animated series just got a Cine-Manga™ makeover...
Lizzie McGuire • Kim Possible
As seen on Disney Channel and Saturdays on ABC Kids
Look for these TOKYOPOP® books in spring 2003!
© Disney. © Mixx Entertainment, Inc. All rights reserved. TOKYOPOP is a registered trademark of Mixx Entertainm

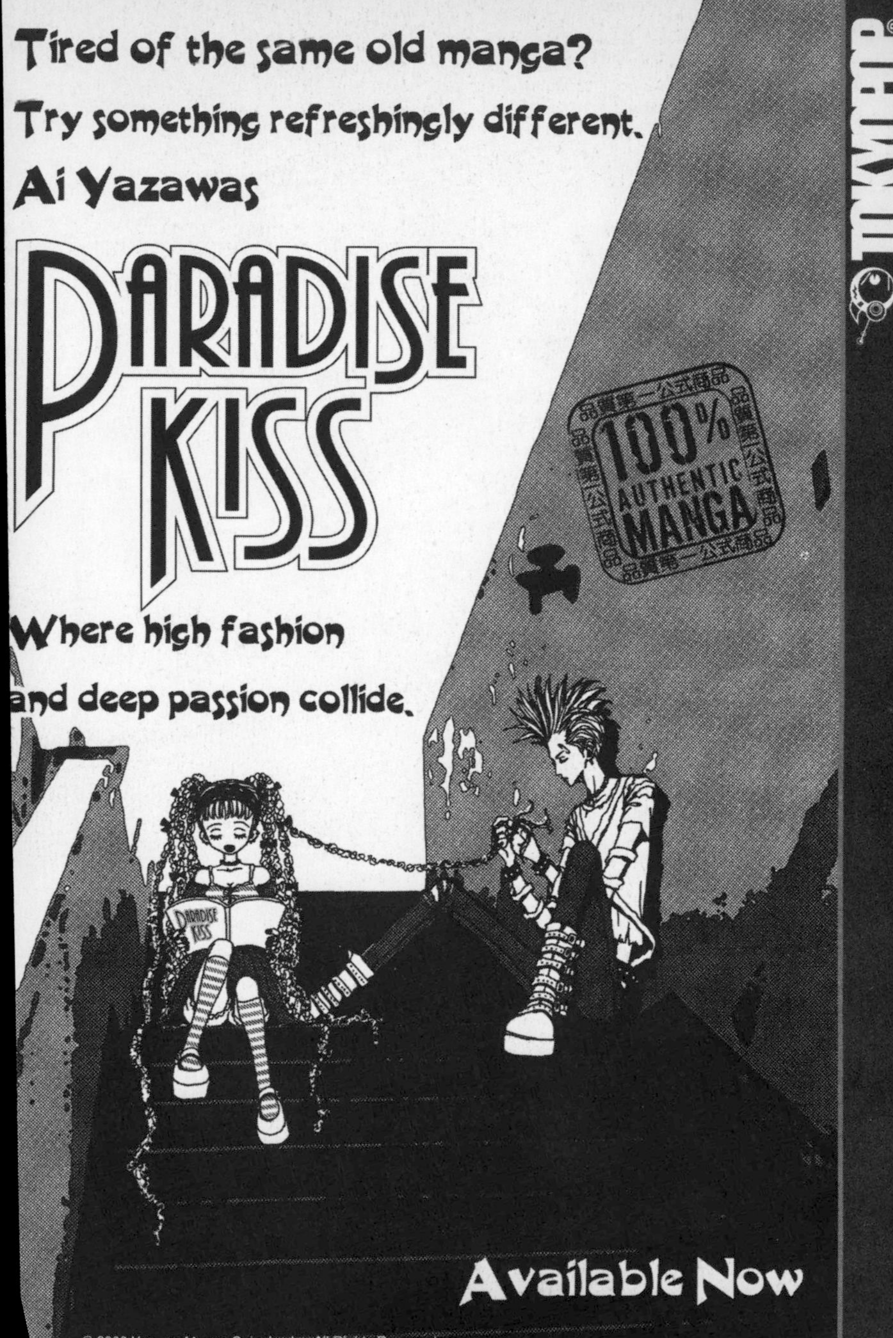
Tired of the same old manga?
Try something refreshingly different.
Ai Yazawas
PARADISE KISS
Where high fashion
and deep passion collide.
100% AUTHENTIC MANGA
品質第一公式商品
TOKYOPOP
Available Now
© 2000 Yazawa Manga Seisakusho, All Rights Reserved.
TOKYOPOP is a registered trademark of Mixx Entertainment Inc.
www.TOKYOPOP.com

STOP!

This is the back of the book.
You wouldn't want to spoil a great ending!

This book is printed "manga-style," in the authentic Japanese right-to-left format. Since none of the artwork has been flipped or altered, readers get to experience the story just as the creator intended. You've been asking for it, so TOKYOPOP® delivered: authentic, hot-off-the-press, and far more fun!

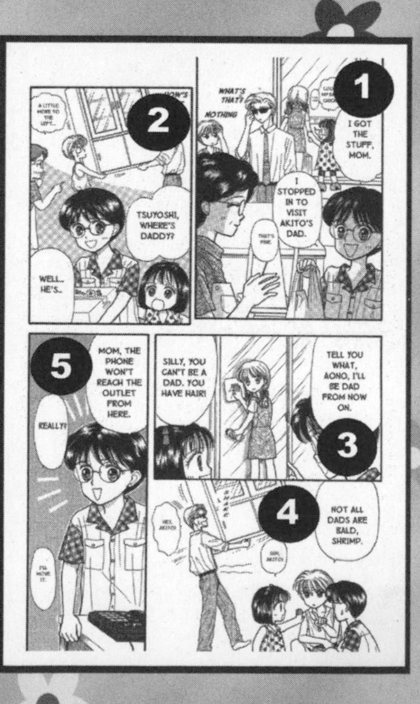

DIRECTIONS

If this is your first time reading manga-style, here's a quick guide to help you understand how it works.

It's easy... just start in the top right panel and follow the numbers. Have fun, and look for more 100% authentic manga from TOKYOPOP®!

100% AUTHENTIC MANGA
品質第一公式商品